The Unsolved Mysteries of Father Marquette's Many Graves

by Jennifer S. McGraw

Pine Stump Publications
Saint Ignace, Michigan

© 2022 Pine Stump Publications

ISBN: 979-8-218-05944-6

Library of Congress Control Number: 2022920977

First Edition 2022

10 9 8 7 6 5 4 3 2 1

Published by Pine Stump Publications
Saint Ignace, Michigan 49781

The cover art is titled "Father Marquette Taking Lessons in Geography From the Indians" by Father Edward Jacker. It can be found within *History of the Diocese of Sault Ste. Marie and Marquette: Containing a Full and Accurate Account of the Development of the Catholic Church in Upper Michigan, with Portraits of Bishops, Priests and Illustrations of Churches Old and New* by Reverend Antoine Ivan Rezek. It is used with permission of the University of Michigan.

No portion of this publication may be reproduced, reprinted, or otherwise copied for distribution purposes without the express written permission of the publisher.

Dedication

For my mother, Suzanne.
Like Father Marquette, her dying wish was to return to the Upper Peninsula. Like Father Marquette, she never made it home.

Thank You

There are so many people to thank for so many different reasons. Many thanks to librarians Skip Schmidt, Barbara Zimmerman, and Jill Eyre from the St. Ignace Public Library and to Kim Kalnbach at Curtis Public Library in Curtis, Michigan. Thanks to Brian Jaeschke at the Widder Library at Mackinac State Historic Parks. Thanks to Alexandra Van Doren and Karen Harag from the Kenneth J. Shouldice Library at Lake Superior State University. Thanks to Les Therrian, formerly with the City of St. Ignace, for discussing found remains in the downtown St. Ignace area. Michelle Sweetser, former University Archivist for Marquette University, kindly answered my questions about Marquette's bones. Thanks to Shirley Sorrels and Tom Wyers for answering questions about Father Marquette's grave and *The Return*. Thanks to Tom Zych from the Toledo Area Aboriginal Research Society for kind permission to use a quote from the Toledo Area Aboriginal Research Bulletin. Thanks to the Michilimackinac Historical Society, and particularly Bill Peek, who recognized and showed me research that was helpful understanding the seventeenth century puzzle that is downtown St. Ignace. Thanks always to Ellen Paquin, Erich T. Doerr, and Wes Maurer from the St. Ignace News for the supportive articles written about this book, and in general, the great job they do promoting and informing about the history of the region. Thanks to the team at Avery Color Studios in Gwinn, Michigan, especially Jodie Verbeke. Thanks to my daughter, Sydney Rosochacki, and my husband, Chris McGraw, for endless reads and rereads. Thanks to John and Joy Hagen for support and encouragement. Thanks to Janette Nelson for editing and cheerleading.

Contents

Location, Timelines 1
1 Background 11
2 Marquette Comes to North America 13
3 The Sault (Mostly the Year 1668) 15
4 Saint Esprit Mission/Sioux (1669-1670/71) 25
5 Return to Sault Sainte Marie/Saint Ignace (1670/71) .. 31
6 Life in Saint Ignace Until May 17, 1673 39
7 The Golden Age 45
8 Journey Begins (May 17, 1673 to July 17, 1673) 49
9 The End of the Journey (July 17, 1673
to the Spring of 1674) 57
10 Results of the Journey 63
11 The Illinois 65
12 Chicago to Ludington 69
13 Bones to Mackinac 71
14 Naming Taboo 75
15 Rediscovery 83
16 Arguments For and Against 89
17 Supporting Oral History Leads to More Questions ... 97
18 What Happened to the Bones 103
19 Modern Findings 107
20 Marquette's Legacy 113
21 The End 117
Footnotes 121
References and Works Cited 131

"From Saint Ignace he departed on his voyage of discovery
of the Mississippi River
… and to Saint Ignace
he was brought back dead."

Keul, Reverend J. A. "Antique Reminiscences of Saint Ignace." *Saint Ignace Enterprise: Woman's Edition*, Saint Ignace Enterprise, 1897, n. p.

Location, Timelines

1534 - French explorer Jacques Cartier traveled to areas of North America. His explorations would launch efforts by the French government to build a colony in North America. This colony would come to be known as New France or Canada.

1611 - The first Catholic missionaries of the Jesuit order made their way to North America, founding missions on the East coast.[1]

1625 - The first Jesuits arrived in Quebec.

1634 - French explorer Jean Nicolet traveled through the Straits of Mackinac to Wisconsin.

1637 - Future Jesuit missionary Jacques Marquette was born.

1639 - A Jesuit mission was built in what is now Ontario, east of Lake Huron and north of Lake Ontario. Living in this area, which was known by the French as Huronia and by the Native American inhabitants as Wendake, were 30,000 Huron Indians. Scattered among the many Huron villages were villages belonging to several Algonquin speaking tribes. Old hostilities soon flamed between the Algonquin and Huron tribes, and their neighbors to the south, a group of several tribes known as the Iroquois.

1641 - The Jesuits sought places to build more missions. At present day Sault Sainte Marie, Michigan, Jesuit Father Charles Raymbault and Father Isaac Jogues founded the Raymbault Mission. Raymbault and Jogues were the first Christian

The Unsolved Mysteries of Father Marquette's Many Graves

missionaries to reach Michigan. Due to illness, they quickly returned eastward, leaving before building any structures.

1648 - The Jesuits found acceptance among the Huron tribe and built eight Huron missions. They also built three missions to serve the nearby Algonquin speaking people.[2] Lumped into the tribal groups the Jesuits referred to as Algonquin were those we would today call the Chippewa or Ojibwa, Mississauga, Winnebago, Potawatomi, Nipissing, Cree, Odawa or Ottawa, and Amikwa, who were also known as the Nez Perce.

Despite building forts around their larger missions, neither the Jesuits nor their Native American parishioners were safe from attacks by the Iroquois. On July 4, 1648, a Jesuit Priest named Antoine Daniel was killed then burned within his own church at St. Joseph, Ontario.[3] He was one of eight Jesuit missionaries among the Huron and their Algonquin neighbors killed between 1640 and 1650. During the same attack, seven hundred Huron were killed or captured by the Iroquois.[4]

1649 - Jesuit Priests Jean de Brebeuf and Gabriel Lalemant were killed on March 16th and 17th, 1649, when one thousand[5] Iroquois with guns and other weapons attacked and burned the Huron villages at Saint Ignace, Ontario and Saint Louis, Ontario. As a result of these hostile actions, fifteen Native American villages east of Lake Huron were abandoned. The Jesuits estimated six thousand[6] people were uprooted and without food, clothes, or other provisions. Many were reduced to eating acorns and roots.

On May 15, 1649, the Jesuits burned and abandoned their mission at Sainte Marie, Ontario.

By 1650, the Jesuits had noted in *Jesuit Relations*, a multiple volume chronicle of their journeys, successes, and failures, that the Algonquin speaking nations and the Huron had begun moving north and west.

Location, Timelines

1650 to 1660 - Those Huron and Algonquins who had not been killed or captured dispersed. Some of the Huron moved to Quebec. Some went west to an island in Green Bay, but then moved, temporarily inhabiting different areas of Wisconsin and eastern Minnesota. The Algonquins followed similar paths.

1656 - The Jesuits again planned to put a mission at what would become Sault Sainte Marie, Michigan. On August 13, 1656, the assigned missionary, Jesuit Leonard Garreau, was shot in the spine by Iroquois on the St. Lawrence River before reaching his destination. The expedition was abandoned.[7]

1658 - Pierre Esprit Radisson and his brother-in-law, Medard Chouart Des Groseilliers, the founders of the Hudson Bay Fur Trading Company, were trading furs on Lake Superior.

1659 - Radisson and Groseilliers built a fort at Chequamegon Bay, a bay at the west end of Lake Superior near present day Ashland, Wisconsin.

1660 - Jesuit Priest Rene Menard traveled Lake Superior in the fall of 1660. He began missionary work in Michigan's Keweenaw Peninsula, calling his post the Sainte Therese Mission.

1661 - While en route to join refugee Huron and Algonquin tribes living at Chequamegon Bay, Wisconsin, Menard became separated from the layman who accompanied and assisted him, Jean Guerin. Guerin had left Menard to walk alone at a portage. Menard was never seen again. Though it's not clear if Menard was killed by hostile forces or simply lost his way, it's said that his possessions were found among the Sioux several years later.[8]

1665 - On October 1, 1665, Jesuit Priest Claude-Jean Allouez arrived at Chequamegon Bay, Wisconsin. He established the Mission of Saint Esprit and built a bark chapel on the shore of Lake Superior between two large villages.[9] The Chequamegon Bay area is referred to by several names in

The Unsolved Mysteries of Father Marquette's Many Graves

history books including La Pointe, the Mission of the Holy Spirit, the Mission of the Holy Ghost, Saint Esprit, or La Pointe du Saint Esprit.

1666 - In Europe, Jacques Marquette received permission from his superiors to travel to North America to serve as a missionary among the Native American tribes. On September 20, 1666, Jacques Marquette landed in Quebec.[10]

1668 - On April 21, 1668, Marquette left the settled areas of New France for the Upper Great Lakes. Once at Sault Sainte Marie, Michigan, he and others constructed a house and church. They surrounded the new buildings with a palisade (fort) for safety.

1669 - A party led by French explorer Jean Pere was sent westward from the settled areas of New France to search for copper near Lake Superior. In the same year, Father Claude Dablon arrived at Sault Sainte Marie, Michigan.

On July 6, 1669, Sulpician Priests Francois Dollier de Casson and Rene Brehant de Galinee left Montreal with explorer Rene-Robert Cavelier de LaSalle.

On September 13, 1669, Marquette took over the Mission of Saint Esprit on Chequamegon Bay in Wisconsin. Father Claude-Jean Allouez had given up in disappointment and choose to start over with a new mission called the Mission of Saint Francois Xavier. This new mission was located on the Fox River, south of Green Bay, Wisconsin.

On September 24, 1669, LaSalle, Dollier, and Galinee briefly met explorer and fur trader Adrien Joliet, brother of Louis Joliet, on the shore of Lake Ontario. He told them of a water route to Lake Huron through the Lower Great Lakes. After LaSalle left the priests on the shore of Lake Ontario, the priests wintered over, but later continued on to explore the Lower Great Lakes, Lake Huron, and the Saint Mary's River.

Location, Timelines

In May of 1670, Galinee and Dollier arrived at Sault Sainte Marie, Michigan where they visited with Dablon and Marquette, who was temporarily in Sault Sainte Marie. Galinee and Dollier departed Sault Saint Marie on May 28, 1670.

1670 - Jesuits Henri Nouvel, Gabriel Druillettes, and Louis Andre arrived at Sault Sainte Marie, Michigan.

During the winter of 1670, Jesuit Father Claude Dablon built a mission at a place identified only as Michilimackinac. Many historians believe this mission was initially built on Mackinac Island, but was moved to the site of present day Saint Ignace, Michigan, a few months later. It was common practice in the 1600s to use the word Michilimackinac to identify Saint Ignace, the region surrounding Saint Ignace, and Mackinac Island.

Shortly afterward, Claude Dablon stated the Jesuits had more than twenty missions in New France, but he clarified that those at Green Bay, Saint Ignace, and Sault Sainte Marie were permanent missions that served as "centers of work".[11] Other Jesuit missions included: A mission among the Mississauga; a mission for the Amikwa (aka the Beaver tribe or Nez Perce) on an island called Ouiebitchiouan (Batchawana Island); the Mission of Saint Simon to the Odawa on the Island of Ekaentouton, now known as Manitoulin Island; a mission on Lake Nipissing in Ontario; and the Mission of Saint Esprit.

On January 27, 1671, the chapel at Sault Sainte Marie, the first built in Michigan, burned down. It was quickly rebuilt. Per several historians, the mission was roughly near the intersection of Water Street and Bingham Avenue, near the site of the obelisk on Water Street. Per *Jesuit Relations 55*:

"A fire, the cause of which could not be discovered, broke out in the chapel last winter, on the 27th of January, 1671, and reduced it entirely to ashes, as well as the house of the

The Unsolved Mysteries of Father Marquette's Many Graves

missionaries, who were able to save from this conflagration nothing but the blessed Sacrament."[12]

1671 - Simon Francois Daumont de St. Lusson, a French government official, traveled to Sault Sainte Marie, Michigan in the spring of 1671. On June 4, 1671, in the presence of over a dozen unconsulted and uninterested tribes, he took possession of the territory around the Great Lakes, proclaiming it to be a possession of the King of France. Several Frenchmen including Canadian born explorer Louis Joliet witnessed the proclamation.[13] Father Claude-Jean Allouez gave a lengthy speech, detailing the reasons the Native Americans should be pleased to be under the wing of the French King. Father Marquette didn't witness the ceremony as he was at the Mission of Saint Esprit on Chequamegon Bay at the far west end of Lake Superior.

Hostilities with the Sioux began to push the Algonquin tribes[14] and the Huron living at the west end of Lake Superior back to the east. Between the fall of 1670 and spring of 1671, the Odawa living near the Mission of Saint Esprit left Chequamegon Bay. On June 14, 1671, Father Marquette left the area with the last of the Huron.[15] Father Marquette went first to Saint Ignace, then to Sault Sainte Marie for a very short time,[16] and then returned to Saint Ignace. At what is now Saint Ignace, Michigan, the Huron began to build a fort. Marquette and his party built a new mission and surrounded it with a palisade or fort.

In the summer of 1671, the Odawa living on Manitoulin Island, east of Drummond Island, went to Montreal to trade for arms to use to attack the Sioux. The Huron joined them in the attack as well as warriors from the Sauk, Fox, and Potawatomi tribes. The Sioux prevailed. The Huron lost a great number of their warriors.

Location, Timelines

1672 - On December 8, 1672, Louis Joliet arrived at Saint Ignace bringing the news that he and Marquette had been tapped to explore areas of the continent west of the Great Lakes.

1673 - On May 17, 1673, Marquette, Joliet, and five French canoemen left on a five month voyage to explore the Mississippi River.

On June 17, 1673, the expedition entered the Mississippi River.

By late fall or early winter in 1673, the party had returned north. Marquette traveled back only as far as Green Bay, Wisconsin. He was sick and could not continue on. Joliet traveled back to Sault Sainte Marie, Michigan and spent the winter. Joliet reached Quebec in the spring of 1674, but lost his maps and notes along with some of his men in a shipwreck at the very end of his journey.

1674 - In the spring of 1674, the missionaries' residence in Sault Sainte Marie, Michigan was burned during a vicious clash with the Sioux.[17] The same year a new chapel was constructed at Saint Ignace.

After being sick throughout the summer, Father Marquette recovered enough to leave Green Bay on October 25, 1674.[18]

1675 - There were over twelve "special missions" by 1675 which included three main missions. Those main missions were located at Green Bay, Sault Sainte Marie, and Saint Ignace. Each of the three main missions had a chapel. In the spring of 1675, Marquette founded the Mission of Immaculate Conception, fulfilling a promise he'd made to build a mission among the Illinois tribes. It was the fifth and final mission where he would serve. His illness soon rebounded. He and two French companions left the Illinois and returned north, hoping to make it to Saint Ignace.

On May 18, 1675, Marquette died on the shore of Lake Michigan near Ludington, Michigan. He was buried there in

The Unsolved Mysteries of Father Marquette's Many Graves

a sandy grave. Two years later, the Kiskakon (Odawa) dug up his grave and brought his bones to Saint Ignace, where they were again interred, this time beneath the floor of the chapel which was built in 1674.

1677 - Marquette's bones were reburied at Saint Ignace on June 9th, 1677.

1689 - Sault Sainte Marie was virtually abandoned by 1689.[19] The population remained strong at Saint Ignace for several more years.

1700 - Robert Livingston,[20] English Secretary of Indian Affairs at Albany, New York, offered one hundred pieces of eight for every Jesuit priest captured and delivered to the English. The Native Americans said no.

Around the end of the century, the population of Saint Ignace began to dwindle. The French had relocated to Detroit. The Huron and some of the Odawa had gone with them. It's commonly believed that sometime between 1703 and 1706, finding few visitors to the mission, Father Etienne de Carheil and Father Joseph Jacques Marest burned the chapel at Saint Ignace to the ground.

1834 - In approximately the same location used by the early Jesuits, a new Catholic church was built on the southern shore of the Saint Mary's River in Sault Sainte Marie, Michigan. It was reported that it was very near an old cemetery, presumed to have been used by the Jesuits.[21]

1856 - On behalf of the Catholic Church, Bishop Frederick Baraga petitioned the U. S. government to be granted the land that had been the site of the early Catholic mission in Sault Sainte Marie, Michigan. This land fronted on the St. Mary's River and was bordered on the west by Fort Brady. The soldiers had constructed several miscellaneous buildings on the claim in the thirty plus years they had occupied the land

Location, Timelines

next door. Nevertheless, a ninety-seven foot by two and three-quarter mile claim was recognized based on knowledge that it had been the site of a Jesuit mission in prior centuries.

1873 - Father Edward Jacker arrived in the Eastern Upper Peninsula in the fall of 1873. He had been assigned to serve in the Native American missions on Mackinac Island and throughout the region. In 1877, he took over the Catholic Church at Saint Ignace.[22]

1877 - Decades passed. Centuries passed. The populations of Saint Ignace waned, but in the late 1800s logging and the coming of the railroad brought about a boom.

In May of 1877, an ancient stone foundation was found in a wooded area near the water front in Saint Ignace. With the guidance of the local priest, Father Edward Jacker, the townspeople excavated the area. During the excavations they found many artifacts of early French origin and several pieces of bone. Then a debate began. Had they found poor Father Marquette? Had his remains been dug up again?

1882 - The citizens of Saint Ignace erected a monument on the site of the discovered stone foundation in 1882. Seven of the excavated bone fragments were buried under the monument. Jacker had reserved another nineteen bone fragments, and contrary to the wishes of some, sent them away to Marquette University.

1970 - Beginning around 1970, archaeologists took an interest in what they called the Marquette Mission site. Several years of study commenced. During this time period, strong evidence surfaced that both supported and refuted the idea that the townspeople had found Marquette's grave.

Background

Father Jacques Marquette lived a brave and adventurous life. As one of the first European missionaries and explorers in North America, he risked his life, most willingly, pressing on until his body gave out. He willed his companions to give him a simple burial under a wooden cross, but his body and bones weren't done with their earthly travels.

After laying in a sandy grave near Ludington, Michigan for two years, his body was exhumed by devoted parishioners. His flesh was separated from his bones and was left in the Ludington area. His bones were transported by canoe to the mission at Saint Ignace. His bones were then received by Catholic missionaries at Saint Ignace de Michilimackinac, only to be buried again, under a primitive church by the sandy shore of Lake Huron.

In 1877, when the townspeople of Saint Ignace discovered thirty-nine fragments of bone in the probable location of Marquette's grave, his bones were thought to have been dug up again. Later, they sent part of these bone fragments to Marquette University where they were carefully stored in the archives department. A few more fragments were given away as souvenirs. Seven fragments found were reburied under a monument to Father Marquette in Saint Ignace. Those seven fragments buried under the monument were eventually dug up again by archaeologists and tested. The results were not as expected.

The Unsolved Mysteries of Father Marquette's Many Graves

Buried. Dug up. Buried. Dug up. Buried. Again dug up. Buried again. The bones of Marquette have been traveling for three and a half centuries. Or have they? This book discusses his life in North America and the unsolved mysteries of Marquette's many graves.

Marquette Comes to North America

In the early 1500s, Europeans discovered an island-filled gulf on the coast of the Atlantic Ocean north of Maine. That gulf narrowed like a funnel and led to the mouth of a wide river. By the mid-1500s, adventurous Frenchmen had traveled up the river, the Saint Lawrence River, for hundreds of miles. There they formed settlements.

French settlers came, attracted by adventure and potential profits from the trade of furs. They were required to be Catholic in order to move to the new country they called New France or Canada.

In addition to the settlers came government officials, merchants, servants, farmers, and missionaries. The missionaries were charged with assuring the continued faith of the Frenchmen as well as the conversion of Native American populations to Catholicism. One of these missionaries was the Jesuit Priest Jacques Marquette.

Jacques Marquette (born June 10, 1637)[23] began to study for the priesthood as a teenager. He was training to become a teacher, but before finishing his schooling, his heart led him to write to his superiors and ask for permission to become a missionary. He asked to be sent to either the West Indies or Canada which was then also known as New France.

About the same time, Father Claude-Jean Allouez, the Jesuit missionary stationed at the Mission of Saint Esprit at the west

The Unsolved Mysteries of Father Marquette's Many Graves

end of Lake Superior, wrote his superiors of a need for more missionaries in his area. He was in charge of the area between what is now Duluth, Minnesota and the Keweenaw Peninsula in Michigan. It was there on the southwestern shore of Lake Superior that the fleeing Huron, the Odawa (Ottawa), and several other tribes had relocated after the fierce Iroquois drove them from their former homes east of Lake Huron.

In 1666, Marquette was excused from his academic studies and sent from France to the developed areas of New France. At the time, the developed areas consisted of only three French villages or towns of more than a few hundred people. These communities, Quebec, Montreal, and Trios Riviers (Three Rivers), were located along a one hundred and fifty mile stretch of the St. Lawrence River, five hundred miles east of Michigan. Marquette stayed there for two years, preparing for assignment in the wilderness. He studied the languages of the tribes assembled for safety in the western areas of the Upper Great Lakes. He learned quickly, mastering both Iroquoian and Algonquin dialects, six or seven in total. This knowledge would allow him to minister to the adaptable, Iroquoian speaking Huron tribe. He also learned Algonquin languages which allowed him to minister to the less interested Odawa, as well as the Ojibwa, Potawatomi, Mississauga, Nipissing, Cree, Amikwa, and Menominee.

In 1668, Marquette left for the western missions; however, instead of being sent to the Mission of Saint Esprit, he was sent to Sault Sainte Marie, Michigan. It was the first of five missions where Marquette would be assigned.

The Sault (Mostly the Year 1668)

The Jesuits first arrived in North America in the early 1600s. The majority of their early missionary work took place east of Lake Huron, along the St. Lawrence River, north and west of the English colonies. In 1636, some of the Jesuits were invited to attend an elaborate Native American funeral ceremony known as the Feast of the Dead. Tribes from hundreds of miles distant were invited. Ojibwa from Sault Sainte Marie attended the ceremony. The Ojibwa asked the Jesuits to build a mission in their village.

In 1641, five years later, the requested mission was launched by Jesuit Priests Isaac Jacques and Charles Raymbault among two thousand[24] Native Americans assembled at Sault Sainte Marie. It was known as the Raymbault Mission. The mission was short-lived. Raymbault became ill and the Jesuits returned east. He died a few months later.

In 1660, nineteen years after the Raymbault Mission was abandoned, Father Rene Menard dared to venture to the Upper Peninsula. He spent a difficult and disappointing winter on the shore of Lake Superior on Keweenaw Bay, living in a shelter made only of fir bows. He then traveled inland to Wisconsin hoping to reach the Huron villages at La Pointe. He became separated from those accompanying him while his traveling companions moved their possessions at a portage. He was never seen again.

The Unsolved Mysteries of Father Marquette's Many Graves

After some false starts by other Jesuit missionaries, Marquette arrived in Sault Sainte Marie in 1668. It had been twenty-seven years since the Raymbault Mission was abandoned.

On the current American side, near the traditional fishing grounds of the resident Ojibwa, the Jesuits erected a chapel and living quarters. These structures were the first constructed for Christian religious purposes in Michigan. To protect the structures, they built a square fortification of twelve foot tall cedar posts. Said Missionary Rene Brehant de Galinee of the Jesuits at Sault Sainte Marie:

"They have had two men in their service since last year, who have built them a pretty little fort, that is to say, a square of cedar posts twelve feet high, with a chapel and house inside the fort."[25]

In his book, *The Story of Sault Ste. Marie and Chippewa County*, historian Stanley Newton deduced that the mission sat roughly at the intersection of Bingham Avenue and Water Street, near the Locks in Sault Saint Marie, Michigan. Though he admitted that he didn't known for sure, he pointed out that a slight rise in terrain matched a description by Father Claude Dablon, and that it was strategically located near the shore and a canoe landing place.[26] There is also an ancient cemetery in this location.

Marquette didn't construct the mission buildings by himself. Jesuit Priests traveled with slaves as well as assistants, Jesuit Brothers, and religious laymen sometimes titled donnés.[27] Donnés were skilled, unpaid laymen who dedicated their lives to be the support staff of the Jesuits. Donné translates to "to give" or "given men". Most of these men acted as construction workers, cooks, farmers, hunters, fishermen, and messengers. They were sometimes sent on transport trips to bring goods to the missions from Quebec or Montreal. Other

The Sault (Mostly the Year 1668)

donné were professionals. Some were surgeons, pharmacists, shoemakers, gunsmiths, metal workers, or others who benefited the missions or the Catholic hospital in Quebec. At Sault Sainte Marie, the Jesuits had at least two donné in Marquette's time.

At times, the Jesuits asked, insisted, or sometimes paid the Native Americans near their missions to build their houses, chapels, palisades, and canoes. Sometimes the Jesuits took over abandoned residences and rebuilt them.

Typically, the Native Americans built structures using bent pole frames covered in bark. Larger structures could stretch to more than one hundred feet in length. Fire pits would be spaced throughout the structures. Smoke simply rose to a hole in the roof, causing dismal, eye-damaging conditions, about which the Jesuits complained repeatedly. The smoke also made the interior of the structures and all of the contents jet black.

Smaller, dome-shaped structures were also used as residences, depending on the tribe of the owner, and if it was intended for long term occupancy.

The frontier buildings belonging to the early Frenchmen were constructed of hewn logs. Primitive log cabins of horizontal logs were one type of construction. Other times, the logs were vertical, lined up in straight lines in the same fashion as the forts built by the French, but likely with smaller logs. The French had fireplaces with chimneys. French houses typically had high pitched roofs so that the second story could be used for storage or for slave quarters.

Typical French residential buildings would have been much smaller than houses built today; however, the Jesuits' house within the Jesuit fort was probably bigger as it was built to house many people at once. It would have provided shelter to the Jesuits and those who accompanied them, as well as

THE UNSOLVED MYSTERIES OF
FATHER MARQUETTE'S MANY GRAVES

any male French visitors or travelers. There were no French women in the Great Lakes until after 1700. The Jesuits probably didn't offer shelter to any Native American wives or companions traveling with trade parties as they initially discouraged marriage between the French men and Native American women.

Native American and French buildings would have been clustered together for safety. The Jesuit house and chapel were within the fort. No doubt, any other buildings were mostly within the Jesuit fort at Sault Sainte Marie or within a nearby Native American fort. Records indicated that in addition to the Jesuit fort, there was at least one Native American fort in Sault Sainte Marie during this time period.

Concern that the village would be attacked was in no way far-fetched. The Iroquois had sent war parties to the U. P. in 1662 at which time they battled the Ojibwa and lost. Though the Ojibwa were victorious, their exposure to attacks would have still been a great concern in 1668. The need for shelter in case of attack would have been in the forefront of the minds of the people.

With the construction of the needed buildings, the mission at Sault Sainte Marie quickly became the center of Jesuit activity in the Upper Great Lakes. The superior missionary resided at Sault Sainte Marie. Missionaries from other Great Lakes missions came and went when seeking a rest or recovering from illness. Sometimes missionaries serving in the many satellite missions would return to Sault Sainte Marie when the villagers they served migrated elsewhere. The tribes often left to go to or from winter hunting grounds, sugar camps, or seek out different sources of food. Some of these missions seemed to be designed as temporary locations for the Jesuits. Writings suggest these transient missions included those serving the Odawas on Manitoulin Island and also missionaries serving the Nipissing and Mississauga on the north shore of Lake

The Sault (Mostly the Year 1668)

Huron. Jesuit missionaries spent long, hard, and hungry winters among these tribes at satellite missions.[28]

Though the Jesuits fought the practice, the Native Americans were nomadic, moving from season to season, as safety demanded, or when food supplies dwindled. The Jesuits sought to change the nomadic nature of the Native Americans. At Sault Sainte Marie the Jesuits began farming and promoting farming to the Native Americans. The Jesuits theorized, if the people focused on farming, winter food supplies would be bolstered, and wandering to winter hunting grounds wouldn't be necessary. This would make the Native Americans more available for religious teachings. This farming also helped the Jesuits feed the "twenty or twenty-five"[29] French who were often about the Jesuit fort.

The Sault Sainte Marie area had many names prior to Marquette's arrival; however, the Jesuits, possibly Marquette himself, who had a great regard for the Virgin Mary, renamed the river on which the Ojibwa village was located the St. Mary's River. They renamed the rapids the Sault (falls in French) Sainte Marie. The Ojibwa people soon were described as being Saulters or Leapers of the Falls in French documents.

The Jesuits admired the Ojibwa's skill in navigating the rapids at Sault Sainte Marie. Per *Jesuit Relations*:

"What is commonly called the Sault is not properly a Sault, or a very high waterfall, but a very violent current of waters from Lake Superior, which, finding themselves checked by a great number of rocks that dispute their passage, form a dangerous cascade of half a league in width, all these waters descending and plunging headlong together, as if by a flight of stairs, over the rocks which bar the whole river."[30]

The Jesuits wrote describing the river and area surrounding Sault Sainte Marie at length. They particularly appreciated the fishery and admired the skills exhibited by the fishermen.

The Unsolved Mysteries of Father Marquette's Many Graves

"It is at the foot of these rapids, and even amid these boiling waters, that extensive fishing is carried on, from spring until winter, of a kind of fish found usually only in Lake Superior and Lake Huron. It is called... whitefish, because in truth it is very white; and it is most excellent, so that it furnishes food, almost by itself, to the greater part of all these peoples."[31]

"Dexterity and strength are needed for this kind of fishing; for one must stand upright in a bark canoe, and there, among the whirlpools, with muscles tense, thrust deep into the water a rod, at the end of which is fastened a net made in the form of a pocket, into which the fish are made to enter. One must look for them as they glide between the rocks... and, when they have been made to enter the net, raise them with a sudden strong pull into the canoe. This is repeated over and over again, six or seven large fish being taken each time, until a load of them is obtained."[32]

Below, Sulpician missionary Rene Brehant de Galinee, described the whitefish fishery and other food sources at Sault Sainte Marie after briefly visiting the Soo in 1670. Four minots equals four U. S. bushels.

"The nation of the Saulteaux, or in Algonkin Waouitikoungka Entaouakk or Ojibways, amongst whom the Fathers are established, live from the melting of the snows until the beginning of winter on the bank of a river nearly half a league wide and three leagues long, by which Lake Superior falls into the Lake of the Hurons. This river forms at this place a rapid so teeming with fish, called whitefish, or in Algonkin attikamegue, that the Indians could easily catch enough to feed 10,000 men. It is true the fishing is so difficult that only Indians can carry it on. No Frenchman has hitherto been able to succeed in it, nor any other Indian than those of this tribe, who are used to this kind of fishing from an early age. But, in short, this fish is so cheap that they give ten or twelve of them for four fingers of tobacco. Each weighs six or seven pounds, but it is so big

The Sault (Mostly the Year 1668)

and so delicate that I know of no fish that approaches it. Sturgeon is caught in this small river, close by, in abundance. Meat is so cheap here that for a pound of glass beads I had four minots[33] of fat entrails of moose, which is the best morsel of the animal. This shows how many these people kill. It is at these places that one gets a beaver robe for a fathom of tobacco, sometimes for a quarter of a pound of powder, sometimes for six knives, sometimes for a fathom of small blue beads, etc. This is the reason why the French go there, notwithstanding the frightful difficulties that are encountered."[34]

According to *Jesuit Relations*, nineteen tribes spent at least part of the year at Sault Sainte Marie, seeking the abundant whitefish. There were around 2,000 people described as Algonquins. The term Algonquin sometimes was used to describe a particular tribe, but here likely meant a language group that included the Ojibwa, Odawa, Potawatomi, Nipissing, Cree, the Noc (Bay de Noc), the Menominee, the Sauk, Foxes, Kickapoo, Miami, Mississauga, Winnipeg, Amikwa/Nez Perce/Beaver Nation, Illinois, and Mascouten, and several other tribal groups which are named but cannot today be identified. The Jesuits said tribes from as far away as Hudson Bay[35] traded at the Soo. Some of these tribes wandered nomadically to such an extent that they had no fixed territory, ranging from the shores of Hudson Bay during the winter to the Great Lakes during the summer.[36]

The Jesuits wrote that the Ojibwa, who were also known as the Chippewa or Saulters, were the actual residents of the area around the St. Mary's River. The other tribes fished or traded there but did not claim the area as their territory.

"The principal and native inhabitants of this district are those who call themselves Pahouitingwach Irini, and whom the French call Saulteurs, because it is they who live at the Sault as in their own country, the others being there only as borrowers. They comprise only a hundred and fifty souls..."[37]

The Unsolved Mysteries of
Father Marquette's Many Graves

Interaction with the nineteen tribes frequenting Sault Sainte Marie provided opportunity for the Jesuits to teach, but also the chance to learn. They soon gathered enough knowledge to surmise that there was a great ocean bay to the north. They thought that it could be part of Hudson Bay. They also learned there was a great river to the west, flowing from north to south, which was three miles wide. It went for such a distance that they could find no one who had ever reached the mouth.

The French were seeking passage to Asia. Learning there was a great river just a few days journey to the west of their missions made them hopeful that river would lead to China. To the Jesuits this was news of an opportunity to reach an untold number of tribes with their message.

Available food and access to the Native American fur hunters attracted the occasional French businessmen and government official to Sault Sainte Marie. Some historians believe that it was in Sault Sainte Marie in 1669 that Marquette met Louis Joliet.

Joliet was born in Quebec in 1645. He had studied to become a priest, but never took his vows. He left his studies at age twenty-two, but kept close ties to the Catholic Church. About a year later, Joliet joined his older brother, Adrien Joliet, exploring and trading furs out of a base at Sault Sainte Marie. They took advantage of the safety of the fort built by the Jesuits, possibly renting rooms, and likely sharing meals with the Jesuits.

Adrien Joliet was three years older than his brother, Louis Joliet. He would no doubt be celebrated today as one of the greatest explorers in Great Lakes history had more of his story been recorded.

On June 13, 1658,[38] while still a teenager, Adrien Joliet was taken prisoner by the Iroquois and held for several months. Three years later, he likely accompanied Jesuit Priest Rene

The Sault (Mostly the Year 1668)

Menard on his mission to the Keweenaw Peninsula. This expedition lasted until 1663. Involvement in this missionary and trading trip meant a glimpse into the earliest profits had by French fur traders. Only a handful of Frenchmen had explored as far inland as the Great Lakes. The financial rewards were great and they were eager to return.

In 1666 and then 1669, partnership papers indicate Adrien Joliet organized and participated in trading trips to the Upper Great Lakes. During his many trips to the Upper Great Lakes, he was known to have spent time at Sault Sainte Marie.

Due to his experience in the western wilderness, Adrien Joliet was tapped by the French government to explore and search for valuable minerals around the Great Lakes. In 1669, after a time at Sault Sainte Marie, Adrien left to explore the area around southern and western Lake Huron. He made it as far as the west end of Lake Ontario when he met a party of Frenchmen that include Sulpician Priests Francois Dollier de Casson and Rene Brehant de Galinee and the noted explorer Rene-Robert LaSalle. Within six months of this trip, Adrien Joliet's wife is listed on official documents as his widow. Adrien Joliet is credited by historians as being the first European to explore the Lower Peninsula of Michigan.

When Adrien left the Upper Great Lakes to explore Lake Huron, many believe Louis Joliet remained at Sault Sainte Marie with the Jesuits, tending to business and trading furs. While there Louis Joliet and Marquette gathered more information about a mysterious, great river in the West from Native Americans who came to the fort to trade. They asked questions, kept notes, and developed maps.

At this time in Canada, Frenchmen were not allowed to travel throughout the wilderness without permission. Marquette sought permission to travel west, hoping to seek out this great river, the Mississippi River. Marquette did receive permission

THE UNSOLVED MYSTERIES OF
FATHER MARQUETTE'S MANY GRAVES

to travel west, but it was not to seek the Mississippi. Marquette was sent to the Mission of Saint Esprit at La Pointe, Wisconsin to serve as missionary to the refugee Huron and Odawa.

Saint Esprit Mission/Sioux (1669-1670/71)

In 1669, a shuffling of positions took place among the Jesuits. Marquette went to the Mission of Saint Esprit and replaced Father Claude-Jean Allouez. Allouez went to the Saint Francis Xavier Mission at Green Bay, Wisconsin. Father Claude Dablon arrived in Sault Sainte Marie and replaced Marquette.

The Mission of Saint Esprit was founded on October 1, 1665 by Jesuit Father Claude-Jean Allouez. It went by many names including Saint Esprit, La Pointe, La Pointe du Saint Esprit, the Mission of the Holy Ghost, the Mission of the Holy Spirit, and the Mission of the Saint Esprit. Sometimes, it was referred to by its location, Chequamegon Bay, a bay on the west end of Lake Superior. The Apostle Islands are located in Chequamegon Bay.

Allouez commented that this assignment brought him contact with twenty[39] different tribes from fifty[40] villages including seven tribes represented within his village.[41] Among those, the Jesuits identified three nations or sub-groups of Odawa living near the refugee Huron at the Mission of Saint Esprit.[42] There were several villages of Illinois[43] to the south and west. Plus there were members of the Ojibwa, Potawatomi, Kickapoo, Sauk, Fox, Miami, and Illinois living there. Many but not all of these people had fled to the area in order to avoid skirmishes with the Iroquois. All feared attack and likely lived in fortified villages (forts).

The Unsolved Mysteries of Father Marquette's Many Graves

The La Pointe area, like Sault Sainte Marie and Saint Ignace, was known to be a rendezvous, a seasonal trading camp and meeting place for tribes from hundreds of miles distant. The fishing, like at Saint Ignace and Sault Sainte Marie, allowed for plentiful food for the assembled tribes. Those camped at Chequamegon Bay rarely harvested game, but lived on fish and corn.

Allouez built a residence and "built a little chapel of bark upon the southwest shore of that rock bound estuary."[44]

At Chequamegon Bay, Allouez found Native Americans who had been instructed by Menard during his attempt to establish a mission on Keweenaw Bay in 1661. Allouez also found many who had never before seen white people.

The following quote describes the tribal diversity the Jesuits found at La Pointe, Wisconsin.

"When Allouez arrived in this polyglot village, October 1, he found there Chippewas, Potawatomi, Kickapoo, Saks, and Foxes, all of them Wisconsin tribes; besides these were Huron, Ottawa, Miami, and Illinois, victims of Iroquois hate who had fled in droves before the westward advances of their merciless tormentors."[45]

Allouez had success in converting the children of the Huron as well as some children of the Algonquin speaking nations. Yet, he complained that he had been given little respect by the adults. He complained that he made little headway eliminating what by his definition was superstitious activity and idol worship. He said:

"God has graciously permitted me to be heard by more than ten different Nations; but I confess that it is necessary, even before daybreak, to entreat him to grant patience for the cheerful endurance of contempt, mockery, importunity, and insolence... "[46]

Saint Esprit Mission/Sioux

Allouez was disappointed in his progress among the Kiskakon, a sub-group of the Odawa. It took three years for the Kiskakon to agree to hear instruction.[47] Allouez persisted and was eventually allowed to baptize their headmen.[48] These roots planted among the Kiskakon would prove important to the history of the Jesuits in the Great Lakes, and notably, later led to their involvement in retrieving Marquette's bones after his death. After a time, Allouez became frustrated and asked to be reassigned to Green Bay, Wisconsin. Marquette arrived to replace him on September 13, 1669.[49]

While at Chequamegon Bay, initially, Marquette like Allouez was frustrated. Marquette like Allouez attempted to eliminate Native American religion, stop sacrifices, and stop those practices he considered indecent. He objected to the ritual sacrifice of dogs and subsequent display about the village of dog carcasses hung on poles. The Jesuits wanted the Native Americans and French to avoid drinking. He and Jesuits throughout North America sought to end the practices of concubinage and polygamy. The Jesuits detested the Native American version of divorce which could be accomplished simply by men abandoning their spouses or by women putting their husband's belongings out of the house (the women owned the houses). The Jesuits also didn't care for a practice among young people which was similar to what we would today refer to as living together before marriage.

The Jesuits attempted to curb the Native American's views on communal ownership of property and personal items. Native American society held that if a person needed something, they helped themselves. The Jesuits saw this as thievery, and tried to impress a more European style of materialism upon the Native Americans.

The Jesuits complained about religious practices organic to Native spiritual life which the Jesuits deemed to be superstitions. Those practices included the following of

27

dreams, Manitous, the use of idols, and dances. Eventually, after a year, Marquette began to report what he deemed to be progress among one of the three Odawa clans at Chequamegon Bay. The Huron, who had been instructed for decades, offered even more promise.

A new problem soon developed. Many of the tribes living near or around the Mission of Saint Esprit had moved westward to escape the raids of the Iroquois, but their new home was in the traditional territory of the Sioux (also known as the Lakota, Dakota, or Nakota). The Sioux soon became as much of a concern as the Iroquois.

The Jesuits seemed to both fear and admire the Sioux, saying they were honorable, kept their word, and never attacked until they were attacked first.[50] They appreciated that the Sioux treated war prisoners more gently than many other tribes, often returning captives unharmed.[51] The Jesuits also described the Sioux as "warlike", and sometimes used the phrase "the Iroquois of the West". Though the Sioux hadn't been armed with guns, they were deadly and fast with bows and arrows.[52]

The Sioux disliked and greatly outnumbered the Odawa, Huron, and their allies. Marquette estimated that the Sioux occupied thirty villages, living in an area stretching from Wisconsin to the Mississippi River. Making matters more difficult, the Sioux spoke a different language than the Iroquoian language spoken by the Huron or the Algonquin language spoken by the Odawa, Chippewa, and others. Marquette helped the relocated tribes including the Odawa and Huron negotiate peace with the Sioux. Marquette sent along presents to seal the deal.[53]

On various occasions of significance, the Native Americans placed high value on and insisted on gift giving. They did this at funerals, as reparations in the case of a wronging or a

Saint Esprit Mission/Sioux

murder, in celebration, and as a way of sealing a deal, like a handshake might be used for a business deal. In this case, the gifts were a token of the peace. Marquette gave the Sioux some religious pictures.

This peace held relatively well until around 1670 when a series of hostile acts on both sides escalated tensions. People on both sides were killed. Some Odawa killed a Sioux chief.[54]

Native American culture believed that victims must exact revenge, practicing what they called "covering the dead" or "drying the tears". An attack was never ignored. This often led to decades-long cycles of violence and revenge raids. Killing a chief couldn't be ignored, but out of respect for Marquette, the Sioux held their revenge attacks until they had returned the religious pictures that he had given them.[55]

What followed was one of the most serious incidents to take place in North America in the seventeenth century. Observers said that the Sioux silently appeared in Marquette's village, bows at full draw. They handed back the gifts that Marquette had given them and melted back into the forest, bows still at full draw.[56] The implication was obvious to the Jesuits and Native Americans alike. Some Odawa and Huron family groups packed their things and left the area immediately. Others chose to wait out the winter. This proved to be a mistake. The Sioux waited for them in the forest. Individuals were killed. Individuals disappeared. Houses were burned. Marquette waited out the winter and returned to Sault Sainte Marie in June of 1671. Soon members of the Huron, Odawa, Chippewa, Mascouten, Potawatomi, Winnebago, Miami, Fox, and some of the Jesuits, including Marquette, were again at Sault Sainte Marie, Michigan[57] or in nearby areas.

"Marquette had succeeded to an uncomfortable berth. Despite his strenuous efforts as a peacemaker, his dusky parishioners soon unwisely quarreled with their western neighbors, the

THE UNSOLVED MYSTERIES OF
FATHER MARQUETTE'S MANY GRAVES

Sioux, with the result that the La Pointe bands, and Marquette with them, were driven like leaves before an autumn blast eastward along the southern shore of the great lake: the Odawas taking up their home in the Manitoulin Islands of Lake Huron, the Hurons accompanying Marquette to the Straits of Mackinac, where he established the mission of Saint Ignace."[58]

By the 1673/74 edition of *Jesuit Relations*, the Mission of Saint Esprit was no longer described as one of the Jesuit missions in the Great Lakes.

Return to Sault Sainte Marie/St. Ignace (1670/71)

In the years 1670 and 1671, the tribes fleeing the Sioux began to assemble in the northeastern Great Lakes, particularly near Sault Sainte Marie, Michigan. The many tribes gathered near Sault Sainte Marie spoke different languages and weren't all friends. They had different traditions and lifestyles. While relative numbers provided safety from both the Iroquois, the enemy from the east, and also the Sioux, the enemy from the west, having all of these people assembled in one small area made for a volatile situation. The tribes were competing for food and space.

Several timely French military victories over the Iroquois had led the Iroquois tribes to plead for peace. Though this overture of peace was not fully extended to the Iroquois' native neighbors, those tribes allied with the French were able to take advantage of the Iroquois losses and spread out.

Different tribal groups took up residence on what the Jesuits referred to as the "Islands of Lake Huron". The Odawa returned to Manitoulin Island, a large island east of Drummond Island. The Odawa had occupied Manitoulin Island around the time of the devastating attack on Saint Marie, Ontario in 1649. The Odawa built the Jesuits a chapel.[59]

An Algonquin tribe called the Amikwa (aka the Beaver Tribe or Nez Perce) moved to the northern shore of Lake Huron, where they fell under the umbrella of a mission called the

The Unsolved Mysteries of Father Marquette's Many Graves

Mission of the Apostles.[60] (This tribe is not the currently identified Nez Perce tribe living in the western United States.) The Mississauga moved to the north shore of Lake Huron.

There were other transient island missions and villages. An old map shows Mission de Saint Simeon (or Saint Simon) on Drummond Island and Manitoulin Island. On Batchawana Island, northwest of Sault Sainte Marie in Whitefish Bay/Lake Superior, the Jesuits asked Native Americans from various nations to build a French fort and chapel.[61]

In 1670, those Huron escaping turmoil with the Sioux, moved to a place the Native Americans referred to as Michilimackinac. It was a place they had lived at some time prior to the arrival of the Europeans. Unfortunately for researchers, in the 17th century, Michilimackinac was a name used to refer to the entire region, Mackinac Island, and also the Saint Ignace area.[62] Because of this lack of context in the Jesuits' statements, confusion exists about specifically where the mission was first built. It's most commonly believed the first mission at Michilimackinac was built by Father Claude Dablon on Mackinac Island, and within a year, the mission was moved to Saint Ignace.

Soon the Jesuits and the tribes which had moved to the north shore and northeastern islands of Lake Huron began to report famine. The Mississauga, Odawa, and Amikwa were reported to be living on tree bark, moss, and acorns. Due to the famine, many of the Odawa families on Manitoulin Island again left. Some joined the Huron at the Straits of Mackinac where they hoped to find an abundance of fish. Others including the Chippewa remained in Sault Sainte Marie.

The missionaries at Sault Sainte Marie reported that an epidemic spread through the village in 1670. It was no doubt one of many. The Jesuits nursed the sick and many recovered. Around that same time ten or twelve Christian Chippewa from

Return to Sault Sainte Marie/St. Ignace

Sault Sainte Marie launched an attack against the Sioux. They lost no warriors, took two prisoners, and killed many Sioux.[63]

While Marquette had been disappointed with his results at La Pointe, the Jesuits at Sault Sainte Marie began to report advances. Those who had been healed during the 1670 epidemic appreciated the Jesuits and the Christian God for their health. The warriors who had attacked the Sioux felt prayer was responsible for their successes.

In 1670, an elderly Jesuit named Gabriel Druillettes (b. 1610) took charge of the mission at Sault Sainte Marie which also served the islands of Lake Huron. Druillettes was exceptional with "cures"[64], a much appreciated skill, as diseases of European origin struck the villages and starvation reduced many including the Jesuits to eating bark and moss. The Jesuits found nursing the sick and performing other services for people increased their favor among the population. The Jesuits pulled teeth. They repaired and provided tools. They nursed the sick. They also provided modern medicines, including opioid based medicines. These medicines were important in providing a pathway for the Jesuits to approach potential converts, and most important to their assignment, it allowed them to baptize those near death.

Despite the good they managed, sometimes even saving lives with their medical knowledge and medicines, Native American people noticed that baptisms seemed to coincide with increases in the number of deaths. Of course, they were right; the arrival of Europeans in part led to an extreme death rate among those living around the Great Lakes in the 1600s. The Jesuits and other Frenchmen, unfortunately, were the source of the diseases killing the Native American people. Notwithstanding the cause, the Jesuits kindly looked after the sick, the women, and children, and invited the Native Americans to seek protection in their fort, rather than a nearby Native American fort.

The Unsolved Mysteries of Father Marquette's Many Graves

In the quote below from *Jesuit Relations*, the Jesuits describe this time in the village at Sault Sainte Marie. The word Nadouessi means the snakes. It was a word the Chippewa used to refer to their enemies the Sioux, but sometimes used the same word to refer to the Iroquois.

"In their reasonable fear of being attacked by the Nadouessi, their enemies, they prefer to dwell near the church, rather than in their own fort. They even wished to place their women and children there for safety, when they went down to Montreal to trade. One of their oldest Captains, named Iskouakite, who is covered with stars [sic] from wounds which he has received either from the Iroquois or from the Nadouessi, endeavored from time to time to increase that confidence by his discourses. He did this especially when Father Gabriel Druillettes called the people with his bell to come to the instruction for he observed that the Father caused the women and girls to pass inside the palisaded enclosure that surrounds the church. "They are truly our Fathers," he said, "These black gowns who protect us and give life to the Sault, by receiving our women and children into their house."[65]

In the spring of 1671, the French presumed their reputation among the tribes had drifted toward favorable. They chose to take advantage of it. That spring French government representative Simon Francois Daumont de Saint Lusson arrived in the Soo. Jesuit Priests Andre, Allouez, Dablon, Druillettes, and several other Frenchmen were there. Pierre Moreau, Jacques Largillier, and Pierre Porteret, men who would be important to Marquette at the end of his life, were also there. Also in attendance were famous young explorers Louis Joliet and Nicolas Perrot.

The French government had sent Perrot throughout the Great Lakes to ask tribes to assemble at Sault Sainte Marie. On May 16, 1671, St. Lusson gathered members of fourteen tribes. With great ceremony, he claimed the Great Lakes region as a

Return to Sault Sainte Marie/St. Ignace

French possession.[66] During the ceremony, Father Claude-Jean Allouez addressed the Native Americans, detailing the benefits of being a subject of the King of France.

"Your canoes hold only four or five men, or, at the very most, ten or twelve. Our ships in France hold four or five hundred, and even as many as a thousand. Other men make war by land, but in such vast numbers that, if drawn up in a double file, they would extend farther than from here to [Michilimackinac], although the distance exceeds twenty leagues. When he attacks, he is more terrible than the thunder: the earth trembles, the air and the sea are set on fire by the discharge of his cannon; while he has been seen amid his squadrons, all covered with the blood of his foes, of whom he has slain so many with his sword that he does not count their scalps, but the rivers of blood which he sets flowing. So many prisoners of war does he lead away that he makes no account of them, letting them go about whither they will, to show that he does not fear them. No one now dares make war upon him, all nations beyond the sea having most submissively sued for peace. From all parts of the world people go to listen to his words and to admire him, and he alone decides all the affairs of the world. What shall I say of his wealth? You count yourselves rich when you have ten or twelve sacks of corn, some hatchets, glass beads, kettles, or other things of that sort. He has towns of his own, more in number than you have people in all these countries five hundred leagues around; while in each town there are warehouses containing enough hatchets to cut down all your forests, kettles to cook all your moose, and glass beads to fill all your cabins."[67]

The Jesuits were pleased by the political changes. They viewed the French King's attention to the region as positive news. Allouez explained that the Native people would henceforth be under the protection of the King's army which was ten thousand strong and well armed. Though most of

The Unsolved Mysteries of Father Marquette's Many Graves

those ten thousand troops were in Europe, those stationed in New France had made headway against the Iroquois. A temporary peace had taken shape. This temporary peace was timely, allowing for migration back to the east when troubles worsened with the Sioux. It allowed the French to leverage their reputation as protectors. It allowed for the tribes to spread throughout the region.

After a brief stay on Mackinac Island, the Huron, along with Jesuit Claude Dablon, and some of the Odawa had moved to East Moran Bay. There the Jesuits built a new mission named Saint Ignace de Michilimackinac. Several months later, Father Marquette joined Dablon.[68] It was the third mission where he would reside and minister.

Again, as they had in Sault Sainte Marie, the Jesuits set about building a chapel, living quarters, and fort.

Fortified towns were necessary due to the ever present threat from the Iroquois and the Sioux. The Iroquois, though temporarily at peace, were a concern to the Jesuits, Odawa, and Huron. Raids by the Sioux were also still unquestionably possible. The Huron and Odawa each constructed forts of their own, and according to written accounts, the head of the bay at Saint Ignace filled with forts made of sturdy logs.

The Jesuit mission and fort were at the center of the bay on the shore. The Huron village and fort were adjacent to the Jesuit mission on the north side. An Odawa fortified village was connected by a common wall to the north side of the Huron village. To the south of those three forts was a group of French houses, and perhaps later the French military fort, Fort de Buade. Fort de Buade was built somewhere in Saint Ignace, but probably many years later. Its location has not been proven. A second Odawa fort was eventually built a distance north of the original Odawa fort. The Odawa eventually also built a fort five miles west of Saint Ignace in the Gros Cap area.

Return to Sault Sainte Marie/St. Ignace

Archaeologists believe they have located the walls of the Huron village in the backyard of what is today the Museum of Ojibwa Culture and Father Marquette Mission Park. They have proven that on the east side the fort stretched nearly to the shore of Lake Huron. The Huron fort encompassed an area of six acres. It contained ten to sixteen long houses, which were estimated to be 25 x 80 feet in size and built of bent poles covered in bark.

Archaeologists have stated that they believe the original adjacent Odawa fort went as far north as Reagan Street. They also stated that they located the bed of a filled in stream which was in the Reagan Street area and defined the northern extent of the Odawa fortified village.

In 1671, the Iroquois burned the villages (forts) at Saint Ignace and first Jesuit mission. The fragile peace began to show signs of cracking.

Hostilities with the Sioux also continued. Within the first year or two after moving to the Saint Ignace area, the Huron joined their new neighbors, the Odawa from Manitoulin Island, to attack the Sioux on their home turf. Per explorer and interpreter Nicolas Perrot, the Odawa traded at Montreal for guns and ammunition, and had a party of one thousand warriors including warriors from the Huron, Odawa, Potawatomi, Fox, and Sauk,[69] but the Sioux prevailed. The losses were great, especially for the local Huron, whose population had dwindled to a mere 380 people by 1673.

Life in Saint Ignace Until May 17, 1673

When Father Jacques Marquette asked to live among the tribes in North America, he had volunteered to serve in a hostile, hazardous, and harsh place, but he and the other Jesuits were driven, and had many goals in mind for their potential converts. They were willing to face great hardships, even death, in order to achieve their goals. They faced many dangers as they tried to change Native American beliefs to mirror those of the French Catholics, and simultaneously, attempted to rein in the French fur traders, who had been given a taste of freedom from French society's rules, and took advantage of the distance from the settled areas of New France.

We are fortunate today to be able to follow the efforts of Marquette and the other Jesuits in a series of books called *Jesuit Relations*. In this seventy-three volume set, around 10,000 pages total, the Jesuits recorded information about their missionary efforts and the lives of their assigned tribes. Though valuable for research, these writings are from the Jesuit perspective and their view point is admittedly often ethnocentric and racially biased.

The eradication of Native American spiritual beliefs was given considerable focus in *Jesuit Relations*. The Jesuits objected to cultural practices which promoted the Native American beliefs in the power of dreams and blackening their faces so that they might have dreams. The Jesuits sought to end all forms of

The Unsolved Mysteries of Father Marquette's Many Graves

Native American spirituality which they deemed to be superstitious. Below are quotes from the Jesuits:

"But I did not trust them, because they are taught from the age of four or five years to blacken their faces, to fast, and to dream of some false God, being led to believe that thus they will be successful in fishing, hunting, and war... In order to... economize their provisions, or to accustom their children to eat only at night... They tell them that then they will dream of the sturgeon, the bear, or the stag Manitou, or of some other similar one, who will make them spear sturgeons or kill bears; and, if they be not old enough to go out hunting or spearing, they still make them fast, by leading them to believe that the hunters and spearers will be successful... These little children have the most ardent longing to kill some animal or spear a fish; hence, if a dreamer be successful for once, they place all their confidence in dreams."[70]

"... they have among them a sort of tradition which makes them believe that, if they have some vision, or rather some dream, they will be fortunate in hunting and war; and that, should they fall into the hands of their enemies, they will escape from them... they accustom them to make long fasts, that they may obtain visions, and may see or hear some spirit in their sleep. They do this with such exactness and austerity as to go 4 or 5 days, and even longer, without eating or drinking anything... "[71]

Over time, the Jesuits were able to convince many of the villagers to abandon their reliance on dreams or visions and instead pray for success. The Native Americans then blamed their losses at war and successes at war, and also their losses and successes at fishing and hunting, on their relationship with God and the Jesuits. If they prayed and then caught fish, the Jesuits reported more attendance in their chapels. If the

LIFE IN SAINT IGNACE UNTIL MAY 17, 1673

opposite occurred, the Jesuits reported a cooling of attitudes, less attendance, even death threats.

The Jesuits also attempted to curb the Native practice of torturing captives. As this was often in retribution for prior acts, and custom required revenge, the Jesuits made little headway. The Jesuits spoke to the captives of Heaven and comforted them. They nursed the wounds the captives received in battle or during tortuous treatment. In many instances, it was recorded that the Jesuits settled for baptizing doomed captives. The episodes of torture were often long lasting, several hours or more in duration. The Jesuits had ample time to baptize captives before the captives were either killed and sometimes eaten, or if the prisoner was extremely lucky, adopted into the tormentors' families.

The following two quotes are from *Jesuit Relations*. They describe the Iroquois torturing two men. Upon a tribe member having a dream which advised the captors to eat the prisoners, the Iroquois ate the men. These extended torture sessions were a common practice of the tribes during that time period including the Great Lakes tribes.

"The red-hot irons were applied to them. One of them, who was burned during the night in a cabin, from his feet to his knees, prayed again to God with me on the following day, while tied to a stake in the public place of the village. I will not repeat here what is already known - that the tortures inflicted upon prisoners of war are horrible. The patience of these poor victims is admirable; but one cannot contemplate without a feeling of horror the sight of their roasting flesh, and of men who devour it like famished dogs."[72]

"One day, when I was passing near the spot where the body of one of those tortured captives was being cut to pieces, I could not help drawing near and inveighing against such brutality. I saw one of these cannibals, who asked for a knife wherewith to cut off an arm. I opposed him... "[73]

The Unsolved Mysteries of Father Marquette's Many Graves

These actions were perpetrated by the local tribes as well as their enemies, the Iroquois and the Sioux, and were part of decades or perhaps centuries of violence and what we would today call terrorism. The thinking was that if the perpetrators could terrorize their enemy enough, the enemy would be fearful and never return to attack their villages. European customs were no more compassionate. Remember that in the 1600s, the Europeans were hanging and pressing to death young women and men thought to be witches in Salem.

The Jesuits tried to intervene on behalf of captives, but showing sympathy for the enemy often caused rifts between village residents and the Jesuits. This endangered the Jesuits.

Human threats, often from those they sought to save, were ever present. Many things the Jesuits did offended the villagers. As can be imagined, simply the constant pressure applied on people to change put the Jesuits in danger. And the Jesuits had a long list of things they would prefer be changed. They wanted an end to gambling, consumption of alcohol, prostitution and the use of prostitutes, and an end to polygamy. They made a fuss about dancing. They opposed nudity and they considered bare ankles on women a form of nudity. They tried to reign in the French fur traders and soldiers as well as their aboriginal parishioners. On some fronts they were successful, while on others, their successes would not come for decades.

Though some writings will state the missionaries were only greeted by love, and no doubt they often were, Jesuits were also frequently scorned, mocked, even threatened by hatchets or knives. Occasionally, Jesuits were beaten. A Native American in one of the villages attempted to cut off the nose of a Jesuit.

There were abundant hardships. The strength and stamina of those living in New France had to be incredible. They would

Life in Saint Ignace Until May 17, 1673

hunt on snowshoes, traveling ninety to one hundred miles[74] in search of game. Via canoe, they would travel forty-five miles a day downstream and half that upstream. On the land crossings between rivers known as portages, the parties' entire outfit of property needed to be carried. Unfortunately, the Jesuits' physical abilities were by far inferior to the Native Americans. The Native Americans sometimes tormented and teased the priests about their physical weakness, sarcastically offering to find children to carry their loads at portages. Below one of the Jesuits explained:

"In addition to all these miseries we met with, at the rapids I used to carry packs as large as possible for my strength; but I often succumbed, and this gave our Indians occasion to laugh at me. They used to make fun of me, saying a child ought to be called to carry me and my baggage."[75]

Those who mocked the Jesuits didn't sarcastically offer to find women to carry the priests' loads. The women often did carry the loads, sometimes with babies strapped on top of the packs on their backs. In the 1600s, Native American women did a great deal of the physical labor in the villages.

In *Jesuit Relations*, the Jesuits also noted many natural hazards. The Jesuits complained of near drownings, and no doubt, their attire, floor-length wool gowns, would have made any fall in the water perilous. Father Allouez told of his canoe swamping, stranding him on a ten foot sandbar in a Wisconsin river for eight days. Jesuit missionaries became lost and spent the night in snowbanks.

They were no safer within their quarters than while traveling. Though tribes often built and/or rebuilt the Jesuits' structures, sometimes the Jesuits' buildings were torn down in malice. There are also statements that one of the Jesuits experienced such affection from the Native Amcricans that they tore off parts of his cabin while he was inside just to look at him.

The Unsolved Mysteries of Father Marquette's Many Graves

Fires frequently menaced the villages, burning down missions and mission houses, sometimes by accident, but at times as punishment inflicted by an enemy. Fires destroyed not just shelters, but hard obtained winter food supplies and necessities such as blankets.

The Jesuits as well as Native Americans often suffered from hunger. While starvation was the cause of death for many Native Americans, sometimes the Jesuits were given food by nearby French traders or Native Americans. At times, there was no food to give. In those times the Jesuits and the Native Americans survived on acorns, tree bark, or as a last resort, a slimy moss called rock tripe. One Jesuit wrote of surviving on a steady diet of crunchy, dried frogs.

Yet, despite these trying, dangerous circumstances, like the Jesuits he served with and those who had gone before him, Marquette relished the hardships and hoped for a chance to die while a missionary. In this he was successful. This young man became the first recorded European to die and be buried in Michigan's soil.

The Golden Age

Threatened by their enemies and battling starvation, misery drove the Huron and part of the Odawa to Michilimackinac in 1670-1671. The time period that followed was somewhat of a golden age for the Jesuits in the Great Lakes. They formed missions, built chapels, and baptized villagers. The priests at Green Bay commented that they were followed everywhere they went, and that children sought them out, even coming barefoot through the snow.

New nations came to meet them. Former parishioners traveled to see them. The Jesuits stated that the parishioners at Michilimackinac included some who had previously received instruction at Green Bay (Saint Francais Xavier), Sault Sainte Marie, and Chequamegon Bay.

Among the resident Huron, Father Marquette's efforts were rewarded. Among the other tribes including some of the Odawa living at Saint Ignace, doubts still lingered. Nonetheless, Marquette reported in a letter to Dablon that he was pleased with the Christian Indians at Saint Ignace. Church attendance was up. Baptisms were up. There was more heed paid to what the Jesuits defined as immoral. More prayers were being said throughout the villages and the chiefs in the village had prohibited nudity.

Throughout *Jesuit Relations*, the Jesuits commented about how successful or unsuccessful hunts or fishing trips could be used to persuade the Native Americans as to God's power. In the first couple of years at Saint Ignace, successful hunting

THE UNSOLVED MYSTERIES OF
FATHER MARQUETTE'S MANY GRAVES

trips aided the Jesuits in convincing the Native Americans that it was God who delivered their success, not their dreams.

"God has aided in a special manner the Hurons who went to hunt; for he led them to places where they killed a great number of bears, stags, beavers, and wildcats. Several bands failed not to observe the directions that I had given them respecting prayers. Dream, to which they formerly had recourse, were looked upon as illusions; and, if they happened to dream of bears, they did not kill any on account of that; on the contrary... "[76]

The Jesuits soon reported that Saint Ignace was the largest and most successful Jesuit mission in the region. Saint Ignace became the base of operations for Jesuit missionaries in the Great Lakes. Dablon, who had been stationed at Saint Ignace, became the Superior of Missions in all of New France. Marquette was given charge of Saint Ignace de Michilimackinac, but Marquette did not wish for a life of easy success in a somewhat developed town. His wishes soon came true. On December 8, 1672, Louis Joliet arrived at Saint Ignace with the news that in the spring of 1673, he and Marquette were to travel westward to find the Mississippi River. Said Marquette of the news:

"I was delighted at this good news, because I saw my plans about to be accomplished, and found myself in the happy necessity of exposing my life for the salvation of all these tribes, and especially of the Illinois, who, when I was at Point Saint Esprit, had begged me very earnestly to bring the word of God among them."[77]

To Marquette, this news was an opportunity. He had long hoped to open new missions, particularly among the Illinois. He assumed he'd encounter the Illinois along the route.

The orders had come from the highest government officials in New France, the Governor of New France, Count Louis

The Golden Age

de Buade de Frontenac, and the Intendant of New France, Jean Talon. The idea that China could be reached via the Mississippi was their utmost hope. Side benefits such as fur trade opportunities, valuable minerals, and relationships with new Native American tribes loomed large.

Marquette's traveling companion, Louis Joliet (born 1645) wasn't chosen because he was a visionary and romantic with an interest in exploring the country for the sake of adventure. He also wasn't chosen because he and Marquette were thought to have been friends. He was an employee of the government and a businessman with high qualifications. He had lived among the Native Americans of the Great Lakes. He spoke several Native American languages. Joliet was among the few Frenchmen who had reached the Upper Great Lakes, traded with the people, and not only understood the hardships of the region, but was able to navigate the fundraising needed for the trip. The government, though making decisions regarding the expedition, offered no funding for it. This had to be done as the trip progressed by trading in furs.

To facilitate this trade, as evidenced by notarized documents, Joliet had formed a trading company with six Frenchmen. They included his brother, Zacharie Joliet (born 1650); Francois de Chavigny La Chevrotiere (born 1650); Jean Plattier (born approximately 1661); Pierre Moreau dit La Taupine (aka the Mole) (born 1639); Jacques Largillier (aka de Castor/the Beaver) (born approximately 1644); and Jean Thiberge/Teberge (born approximately 1642). Little is written of these men to whom so much credit is due.

These men weren't new to the fur trade or to the Great Lakes region. Moreau had been a soldier in the garrison at Quebec. Other partners had been west two years prior and had been witnesses when St. Lusson audaciously claimed the region for the French king. Some of these men had previously been partners of Louis Joliet's deceased brother, Adrien Joliet.

The Unsolved Mysteries of
Father Marquette's Many Graves

Marquette and Joliet prepared for the trip throughout the winter months. They secured canoes and provisions. On May 17, 1673, Joliet, Marquette and five men left to find the Mississippi River. No known written record tells us which men accompanied Marquette and Joliet on their journey, but no doubt, the partnership documents previously discussed are a clue to the identities of the five canoemen.

Journey Begins (May 17, 1673 to July 17, 1673)

On May 17, 1673, after waiting for spring to break, Marquette, Louis Joliet, and five Frenchmen left Saint Ignace in two birch bark canoes. They took with them meager supplies including clothes, beaver robes, religious books, notebooks, a compass, and a sundial.[78]

Canoes designed to hold multiple paddlers and thousands of pounds of cargo were the primary source of transportation during the fur trade. At times, they were fitted with sails to increase their speed. Travelers hugged the shore in order to safeguard against swift moving Great Lakes storms. The first sailing ship wouldn't reach the Upper Great Lakes until after Marquette's death.

It wasn't a trip of luxury. The Great Lakes were dangerous. The bugs were horrendous. Food was gathered on the way with the exception of some corn and smoked meat. Marquette described, "the labor of paddling from morning to night."[79]

Local lore says that Epoufette on the north shore of Lake Michigan was the first stop for the night. Epoufette is said by some to mean "the place of rest". Epoufette was probably one of many traditional camping places which had available fresh water and level, dry ground. They would have pulled into shore after a hard day and set up a camp, built a fire, and hung a pot over it. Unless the travelers were taken in for the night by Native groups, their sleeping places would have been on the ground, perhaps under the canoe. They broke camp in the morning and paddled.

Within a few days, the party arrived at a village inhabited by the Menominee tribe. Marquette had met the Menominee before, in fact, they had been receiving religious instruction from the Jesuits for some time. The Menominee warned the travelers against their journey to find the Mississippi. Marquette responded with typical determination. Following, he describes their conversation in *Jesuit Relations*:

"They were greatly surprised to hear it, and did their best to dissuade me. They represented to me that I would meet Nations who never show mercy to strangers, but break their heads without any cause; and that war was kindled between various peoples who dwelt upon our route, which exposed us to the further manifest danger of being killed by the bands of warriors who are ever in the field."[80]

"They also said that the great river was very dangerous, when one does not know the difficult places; that it was full of horrible monsters, which devoured men and canoes together; that there was even a demon, who was heard from a great distance, who barred the way, and swallowed up all who ventured to approach him. Finally [they said that] the heat was so excessive in those countries that it would inevitably cause our death."[81]

"I thanked them for the good advice that they gave me, but told them that I could not follow it, because the salvation of souls was at stake, for which I would be delighted to give my life; that I scoffed at the alleged demon; that we would easily defend ourselves against those marine monsters; and, moreover, that we would be on our guard to avoid the other dangers with which they threatened us. After making them pray to God, and giving them some instruction, I separated from them."[82]

Journey Begins

Between the Menominee village and the Mississippi, they traveled through Green Bay and into the mouth of the Fox River. Just off Green Bay on the first set of rapids on the Fox River was the Jesuit mission, St. Francis Xavier Mission. The location, like Sault Sainte Marie, Michigan and Saint Ignace, Michigan, was a traditional seasonal camp site used by several Native American tribes. The tribes were drawn year after year to an abundance of fish found seasonally along these rapids, which were named by the Jesuits the Rapids des Peres (De Pere) or the Rapids of the Fathers. This mission was considered one of the three main missions in the Great Lakes in 1673. There they met with the Mascouten, Miami, and Kickapoo on June 7th. There is no reference to meeting with the Jesuits who resided there.

The travelers soon reached the limits of the area previously explored by the French.

One month into the journey, on June 17, 1673, Joliet and Marquette's party first laid eyes on the great Mississippi River. They turned south.

As the explorers descended the river, they were vigilant. They had been warned that lower on the river the tribes were constantly at war with one another. They realized that there was a likelihood of attack by hostile tribes.

"We continued to advance, but, as we knew not whither we were going, for we had proceeded over one hundred leagues without discovering anything except animals and birds, we kept well on our guard. On this account, we make only a small fire on land, toward evening, to cook our meals; and, after supper, we remove ourselves as far from it as possible, and pass the night in our canoes, which we anchor in the river at some distance from the shore. This does not prevent us from always posting one of the party as a sentinel, for fear of a surprise."[83]

The Unsolved Mysteries of Father Marquette's Many Graves

Using their sails, they created tent-like structures on their canoes. These protected the explorers from the vicious mosquitoes at night and the hot sun during the day.

After seeing no people for more than three hundred miles, they discovered and followed a path far from the Mississippi and found an Illinois village. Marquette had a fondness for the Illinois, perhaps, in part, due to his affection for an Illinois slave he had been given at the Mission of Saint Esprit. At this stop on the trip, the Illinois presented Marquette with another Native American slave, a young boy. All of the ethnic groups in the region kept captured Native Americans from distant tribes as slaves.

Despite the fact that the Illinois traded heavily in enslaved Native Americans, Marquette described the Illinois as docile, gentle, and hospitable. The Illinois held a great feast, celebrating the arrival of the Frenchmen.

"The council was followed by a great feast, consisting of four dishes, ... a great wooden platter full of sagamite, that is to say, meal of Indian corn boiled in water, and seasoned with fat. The master of ceremonies filled a spoon with sagamite three or four times, and put it to my mouth as if I were a little child. He did the same to Monsieur Joliet. As a second course, he caused a second platter to be brought, on which were three fish. He took some pieces of them, removed the bones therefrom, and, after blowing upon them to cool them, he put them in our mouths as one would give food to a bird. For the third course, they brought a large dog, that had just been killed; but, when they learned that we did not eat this meat, they removed it from before us. Finally, the fourth course was a piece of wild ox, the fattest morsels of which were placed in our mouths."[84]

It has been stated previously in this text that the travelers had many things to fear including hostile tribes, drowning, and

Journey Begins

hunger. Perhaps though, the immediately preceding passage describes what may have been the most unsafe aspect of the trip for Marquette; he began to have stomach problems, maybe due to unsanitary conditions.

During their stay with the Illinois, the Illinois gave Marquette a calumet or peace pipe. It signified their trust in the missionary and their commitment to the French. The calumet was used as a passport or white flag, signifying peaceful intentions. It was normally universally accepted among the North American Indians. Below, early fur trader and interpreter, Nicolas Perrot explained the significance of the calumet.

"The calumet halts the warriors belonging to the tribe of those who have sung it, and arrests the vengeance which they could lawfully take for their tribesmen who have been slain. The calumet also compels the suspension of hostilities and secures the reception of deputies from hostile tribes who undertake to visit those whose people have been recently slain by theirs. It is, in one word, the calumet which has authority to confirm everything, and which renders solemn oaths binding."[85]

"They have so much respect and veneration for it that he who has violated the law of the calumet is regarded by them as disloyal and traitorous; they assert that he has committed a crime which cannot be pardoned. In former times this was the obstinate contention of the [people], and they are still of the same opinion; but that does not hinder them from committing acts of treachery while employing the calumet. Those of the prairies have the utmost attachment for it, and regard it as a sacred thing. Never did they betray the pledge that they had given to those who sang it... That would be the basest of all traitorous acts, because it would break the calumet in pieces and disrupt the union which had been contracted through its agency."[86]

And, below the Jesuits discuss the importance of the calumet:

THE UNSOLVED MYSTERIES OF
FATHER MARQUETTE'S MANY GRAVES

"... It has but to be carried upon one's person, and displayed, to enable one to walk safely through the midst of enemies, who, in the hottest of the fight, lay down their arms when it is shown."[87]

Marquette and Joliet's party recognized that simply possessing the calumet could save their lives. The Illinois told them that the tribes that resided further south on the Mississippi were hostile. Soon after leaving the Illinois, they discovered their reception among the tribes residing on the river cooled, and then became unsafe. If not for displaying the calumet, the explorers might have been killed.

The general direction the river was running confirmed they were headed toward the Gulf of Mexico and Spanish territory. Marquette and Joliet were already leery of this. Several years prior, Marquette had been told that Frenchmen with "large canoes with sails"[88] lived at the mouth of the Mississippi. Prior to embarking, they had developed several theories as to where the great river went; however, they could figure no way the men discussed could be Frenchmen. They surmised that they were heading into the territory of the Spanish. They were apprehensive. It wasn't that they expected to run into Spanish soldiers. Oddly, though the Spanish explorer Hernando de Soto had mapped the Gulf of Mexico one hundred years before Marquette and Joliet's trip, for some reason relating to the swampy terrain at the mouth of the Mississippi, the Spanish had never identified the mouth. They had hoped, however, to avoid the Spanish allies. They knew the Spanish had guns and may have armed their allies with guns.

"Then the Father and Sieur Joliet deliberated as to what they should do, that is, if it were advisable to go on, they felt certain that, if they advanced farther, they would fling themselves into the hands of the Spaniards of Florida, and would expose the French who accompanied them to the manifest danger of losing their lives. Moreover, they would lose the results of

Journey Begins

their voyage, and could not give any information regarding it, if they were detained as prisoners, as they probably would be, if they fell into the hands of Europeans."[89]

They had enough evidence to conclude that the Mississippi terminated at the Gulf of Mexico. They were risking their lives, and they worried that their discoveries, journals, and maps could be captured, and the knowledge gained from such a treacherous journey could be lost. After a thousand miles of canoe travel, near the mouth of the Arkansas River, six hundred miles from the gulf, Marquette and Joliet became concerned enough to end their trip. On July 17th, 1673, the explorers turned north.

The End of the Journey (July 17, 1673 to the Spring of 1674)

Again, the fearless explorers reached their home range, finding their way to the mission of Saint Francis Xavier at De Pere, Wisconsin in September of 1673. This was the place they had left Lake Michigan, and the relative safety of the known area surrounding Green Bay. While Marquette remained in Wisconsin, Joliet returned east, heading to Sault Sainte Marie, and then to Montreal in the spring of 1674. After traveling thousands of miles by canoe without an incident, his canoe overturned in rapids near Montreal. Two of his men and a child slave were drowned. The notes taken by Joliet were lost. Fortunately, a second copy of his notes and maps had been left at the Jesuit mission in Sault Sainte Marie.

His superiors in Montreal and Quebec were disappointed. They were designing a colony around his team's findings. They understood the irony, however, that this disaster struck after Joliet had successfully navigated forty sets of rapids and thousands of miles of uncharted wilderness.[90]

Immediately, he set about reconstructing his notes and maps from memory. It's a good thing as the backup copies of his notes and maps, left for safe keeping with the Jesuits in Sault Sainte Marie, Michigan, were also destroyed in the spring of 1674 in a brutal event.[91]

The Unsolved Mysteries of Father Marquette's Many Graves

In 1674, the Sioux sent ambassadors to Sault Sainte Marie seeking peace. Instead butchery and mayhem resulted. The missionaries' house was destroyed. The chapel was nearly destroyed. All of the Sioux ambassadors were killed along with two of three women who accompanied them and many others.

Below, the altercation is described in *Jesuit Relations 58*. In this description, the Sioux are referred to by Nadouessi or Nadoissi. The Cree are referred to as Kilistinons. The Mississauga are an Algonquin tribe who lived on the northern shores of Lake Superior or Lake Huron. The Ojibwa living at Sault Sainte Marie are referred to as Sauteurs. The Odawa are referred to as Outaouac, but in this text, Outaouac means Odawa, but is being used as an all-inclusive term describing all of the Algonquin speaking tribes of the region. Historic quotes can sometimes be culturally insensitive and some of these are. In general, statements made by the explorers, soldiers, and Jesuits are sometimes blunt, racist, patronizing, and ethnocentric. Nevertheless, word choice in original statements can sometimes be revealing. As such, the quotes have not been altered.

"The Nadouessi, a nation exceedingly numerous and warlike, were the common enemies of all the savages included under the name of Outaouac, or upper Algonquins. They even pushed forward their arms vigorously toward the north; and, making war on the Kilistinons who dwell there... "

"[The Sioux] use, among other weapons, knives of stone. Of these, they always carry two, one attached to the girdle, the other suspended by the hair. However, a band of warriors from Sainte Marie du Sault, having surprised them in their own country and taken eighty of them prisoners, compelled them to sue for peace. For this purpose, they sent to the Sault ten of the most daring among them, to negotiate it. They were received with joy, as soon as the object of their coming was understood."

The End Of The Journey

"It was the Kilistinons alone, who had lately arrived, save some others named Mississaugas, who not only expressed their dissatisfaction in the matter, but resolved moreover to prevent the peace from being concluded. They even determined to massacre the ten ambassadors, a proceeding which made it necessary that the latter, in order to ensure their safety, should be placed in the French house, which had been erected for the convenience of the missionaries... "

"Meanwhile, the savages assembled at the French house, part of them to conclude the peace with the Nadoessi, others to obstruct its conclusion. Everything imaginable was done to prevent those who went in from carrying arms; but, as the crowd was very great, five or six slipped in without having their knives taken from them. It was one of these latter, a Kilistinon by nation, who began all the disturbance that ensued. Approaching a Nadoessi, knife in hand, he said to him, "Thou art afraid."

"The Nadoessi, undismayed, replied to him in a haughty tone, and with a confident air, "If thou thinkest that I tremble, strike straight at the heart." Then, feeling himself struck, he cried out to those of his nation, "They are killing us, my brothers." At these words, the men, stirred up to vengeance... arose, and struck with their knives at all the assembled savages, without making any distinction between Kilistinons and Sauteurs, believing that they had all equally conspired in the design to assassinate them."

"It was not very difficult for them to accomplish a great carnage in a short time, when we consider that they found that multitude unarmed, and expecting anything but an attack of that kind. The Kilistinon who had begun the quarrel was among the first to be stabbed; and, he, with several others, fell dead on the spot. Afterward, the Nadoessi posted themselves at the door of the house to guard it, and to stab those who would have taken to flight; but, seeing that many had already escaped and gone in search of arms, they closed the door against these, resolved to defend themselves to the last breath. In fact, they stationed themselves at the windows; and as, by chance, they had found some guns, with powder and ball, they used these to disperse their enemies... "

"They killed, in this way, some of those who ventured too close; but in spite of their efforts, some others came close to the house. These men, having piled up against it some straw and some birch-bark canoes, set fire to them, which at once placed them in danger of being consumed in the flames. It was this that drove them to give a last proof of their courage."[92]

The Sioux eventually were driven from the missionaries' house by the fire. They ran quickly to a nearby vertical log cabin. This was a better fortification. They continued to shoot and bring down those who approached and lasted until their shot and powder ran out. Only a single female slave was spared among the Sioux party. The fire destroyed the missionaries' house and nearly destroyed the church.

"It was a horrible spectacle to see so many dead, and so much blood shed in so small a space: and horrible to hear the cries of those who warmed to the battle, and the groans of the wounded... "[93]

The Jesuits said that forty local tribesmen were killed or wounded including several prominent men. Again, hopes for peace were dashed. Again, as they had during the exodus of Chequamegon Bay, the tribes feared retribution from the powerful Sioux and fled.

The prior quotes describing the massacre at Sault Sainte Marie are from *Jesuit Relations*. Several old texts, but not *Jesuit Relations*, state that Jesuit Brother Louis le Boesme[94] was involved in the altercation with the Sioux.

Le Boesme was a long time donné. He had entered the service of the Jesuits as a teenager and worked for decades in hostile

The End Of The Journey

Iroquois territory. Jesuits and volunteers who had been in his acquaintance had been tortured and killed. A statement in *Jesuit Relations 42* may be interpreted to say that in 1655, he was shot twice in a clash with the Iroquois.[95] Bravely, he continued his work with the missionaries for his entire adult life.

Many of the French who traveled west were just teenagers. Le Boesme was a mature 36 year old when he accompanied Marquette to Sault Sainte Marie. Once there, he was put in charge of what the Jesuits referred to as the temporal affairs of the mission at Sault Sainte Marie. This meant it was his job to care for the house and any other buildings that were claimed or built by the Jesuits. He seemed to be a man of many skills. In different sources he is listed as an armorer, jeweler, gunsmith, or blacksmith.

According to some sources, when it became obvious that the Sioux would not relent, Le Boesme feared that the structure they hid in would be burned. There was a fortune in furs stored in the second story which might be destroyed. He offered a solution. He allowed the Sault-area warriors to use a cannon. The cannon was shot through the building.[96] This killed the remaining Sioux.[97] Below the affair was described in *Jesuit Relations*:

"We have also at Sainte Marie one of our lay brethren; he has… charge of that house, which was burned a second time in consequence of a sanguinary affray, in which over forty savages cruelly slaughtered one another. It is a wonder that two of ours, who were there, were not included in that butchery… "[98]

Jesuit Relations doesn't mention Brother Le Boesme's involvement, but several other sources state that government officials were angered that Le Boesme volunteered the cannon. It's possible that the Jesuits didn't want Le Boesme's[99] involvement to be widely known. Any widespread knowledge of a Frenchman's involvement in the

THE UNSOLVED MYSTERIES OF
FATHER MARQUETTE'S MANY GRAVES

event endangered the lives of the Jesuits and other Frenchmen throughout the Great Lakes.

The Jesuits and Native Americans alike had worked for years toward peace between the Sault Sainte Marie tribes and the Sioux. Many felt they were on the edge of finalizing a peace deal between the Sioux and Algonquin nations. Instead, hostilities renewed and soon the bloody war resumed.

Results of the Journey

Soon after the massacre at Sault Sainte Marie, the Jesuits from Green Bay reported war dead in nearby villages from clashes with the Sioux. Father Marquette and Marquette's notes from the voyage down the Mississippi River remained safe at the Mission of Saint Francis Xavier and his papers eventually did reach government officials. The reconstructed notes of Joliet and Marquette's map and journal were some of the most important documents produced in North America in the 1600s.

The journey helped develop a new understanding of North American geography. The French then knew that the Mississippi would not directly lead them to China; however, they still hoped the Missouri River might be a viable trek.

On the way north, the explorers left the Mississippi River, canoeing up the Illinois River to the Des Plaines River, eventually traveling along the Chicago River, and portaging to Lake Michigan. From this detour, the French learned that with the addition of some canals, via the Mississippi, they could open up a shipping route from Quebec to the Gulf of Mexico by going through Lake Erie, Lake Huron, and Lake Michigan.

The explorers reported finding beautiful, game-filled, treeless lands surrounding the Mississippi, and admired the fertile soil of the area. They recognized the capacity of this area to support farms, something the French settlers had yet to find much success with, something necessary to the success of New

The Unsolved Mysteries of Father Marquette's Many Graves

France. They appreciated the time savings a future farmer might find, explaining that, "A settler would not there spend ten years in cutting down and burning the trees; on the very day of his arrival, he could put his plow into the ground."[100]

The explorers discovered an extensive capacity to expand the fur trade toward the west, and to hem in the English by constructing villages and forts west of the colonies of the English. In addition, the attitudes toward the French of eighty tribes living along the Mississippi were recorded.[101]

Once in Quebec, Joliet asked for permission to return to the explored area surrounding the Mississippi River to build French settlements, but he would never again venture west of the Great Lakes. In the meantime, Marquette continued his recovery at Green Bay.

In 1674, Marquette was listed among the Jesuit missionaries assigned to the Saint Francis Xavier Mission at Green Bay along with Jesuit Fathers Allouez, Andre, and Silvy. It was the fourth mission where Marquette was assigned.

In the vicinity of Green Bay and the Fox and Wolf Rivers in Wisconsin was a substantial mission with several smaller missions. Native Americans from at least twelve different tribes lived in five or more villages, a few miles apart. Those tribes, whose home ranges stretched far into Wisconsin, had no safety from Sioux, or the Iroquois, who had then recently attacked the tribes in Wisconsin.

Returning to the established Saint Francis Xavier mission gave Marquette a chance for a needed rest. He rested and worked on his journals. He also made plans to establish a mission among the Illinois.

After more than a year recovering at Green Bay, Marquette felt well enough to head south to found a mission among the Illinois.

The Illinois

While at Chequamegon Bay, Marquette had met and bonded with members of the Illinois tribe from the Chicago area. They asked Marquette to visit them and he had made plans to do so. The Odawa had given Marquette an Illinois slave. The slave taught him to converse in the Illinois language which helped him to prepare.

Marquette's trip to the Mississippi had given him the chance to visit several Illinois villages. He learned the Illinois still wished to have a missionary live among them; however, throughout the end of 1673 and through most of 1674, Marquette fought illness. Though still sick, Marquette left Green Bay on October 25th, 1674, in order to establish a mission among the Kaskaskia, a subtribe of the Illinois. The French often lumped tribes into groups according to the languages they spoke. To the Jesuits, the Illinois included the Miami, Kaskaskia, Cahokia, Peoria, Tamaoa, and the Wea tribes.

Jesuit Relations tells of the extended battle Marquette had with "the bloody flux" or bloody dysentery. When in October of 1674, Marquette had recovered enough strength to continue on to the Illinois, two Frenchmen accompanied him. They canoed to a portage at Sturgeon Bay, where they joined a party of Illinois. Because of harsh weather, they didn't reach the south end of Lake Michigan until December 4th, 1674. Once at the south end of Lake Michigan, they were unable to go on due to Marquette's health. He and his companions, Pierre

The Unsolved Mysteries of Father Marquette's Many Graves

Porteret and Jacques Largillier, took shelter on the Chicago River portage at the present site of the City of Chicago.

In January of 1675, news of Marquette's illness and confinement reached a nearby French trading party. Pierre Moreau dit Taupine, a former business partner of Adrien Joliet, was living not far distant. Moreau had been at Sault Sainte Marie with Louis Joliet and Marquette's two companions, Jacques Largillier and Pierre Porteret, when St. Lusson had claimed the territory for the King of France. In addition, Moreau and Largillier were both partners in the company that Louis Joliet had formed prior to undertaking the journey to the Mississippi.

Among Moreau's party was a surgeon, one of only a handful of surgeons, or barber-surgeons, known to have been in New France in the 1600s. (In the 1665-66 census, there were five surgeons in New France.) The surgeon checked on Marquette during his stay at the Chicago Portage. Unfortunately, the surgeon is not named in *Jesuit Relations*.

During the four months Marquette was delayed at the portage, the surgeon, the few French in the area, and the Illinois tried to keep Marquette's cabin supplied, sending blueberries, dried pumpkin, buffalo tongues, corn, and for his comfort, beaver skins.

Even while sick, Marquette busily promoted peace among nearby tribes, discouraging the Illinois from warring with the nearby Miami. He ministered to those French and Native Americans who visited him in his illness. He promised he would soon visit the Illinois in their villages.

Even so, his two companions, Jacques Largillier and Pierre Porteret, were at times his only companions at this place of residence which they referred to as "the portage". They hunted and cared for Marquette. They explored the area, finding Native American villages within short distances.

The Illinois

They traded for food, or at least tried, because at times the surrounding villages also complained of hunger.

Jesuit Relations states that one of Marquette's two French companions had accompanied Marquette and Joliet down the Mississippi. Unfortunately, it does not say which one.[102] Many presume that it was Jacques Largillier as he was a partner in the company formed to raise funds for the trip. Largillier was well qualified. As a former business partner of Adrien Joliet, he had contracted to trade around the Great Lakes for at least four seasons prior to the expedition to the Mississippi River.

Toward the end of March in 1675, an unexpected spring flood created a treacherous situation for Marquette and the travelers. They tied their possessions in treetops and evacuated to a nearby hill. Floodwaters rose twelve feet. Luckily, Marquette's health had been improving. They took it as a sign to leave the area of the portage, and finally reached the Illinois villages on April 8, 1675. There Marquette founded the Mission of Immaculate Conception, the fifth and final mission where Marquette would serve. In *Jesuit Relations*, Father Claude Dablon, the Superior of the Jesuit Missionaries, wrote that the Illinois received Marquette fondly, assembling in great numbers to hear him.

"… having given instruction in the cabins, which were always filled with a great crowd of people, he resolved to address all in public, in a general assembly which he called together in the open air, the cabins being too small to contain all the people. It was a beautiful prairie, close to a village, which was selected for the great council; this was adorned, after the fashion of the country, by covering it with mats and bearskins… The audience was composed of 500 chiefs and elders, seated in a circle around the father, and of all the young men, who remained standing. They numbered more than fifteen hundred men, without counting the women and children, who are always numerous, the village being composed of five hundred or six hundred fires... On the third day after... he took possession of that land in the name of Jesus Christ, and gave to that mission the name of the Immaculate Conception of the Blessed Virgin."[103]

Though he was experiencing great success, he could not keep the dysentery under control. Faced with the knowledge that he would die, Marquette made the decision to leave the new mission of Immaculate Conception to again return to Michilimackinac. Out of respect for Marquette, the Illinois carried his belongings for the first ninety miles.[104]

Chicago to Ludington

Marquette left Chicago with his two companions. Some believe he was returning to Saint Ignace in order to attend a gathering[105] of all of the Catholic missionaries from the area. Some believe he knew he was soon to perish, and wanted it to be at the mission he so loved. Maybe he felt the other missionaries were skillful enough at medicine that they might save him. Perhaps, he knew he would soon die and hoped to reach Michilimackinac in order to be buried in a Catholic cemetery. Perhaps, all of these things are true.

They traveled along the western shore of the Lower Peninsula of Michigan. Part of the time, he rode in the bottom of the canoe. It became evident that Marquette would not live long enough to again see the Mission of Saint Ignace. Before he became too weak to give instructions, he asked that they put the canoe ashore near the mouth of a river near Ludington, Michigan. There was a small lake which he thought would serve as a landmark, making his grave site identifiable in the future.

The two men built a shelter for Marquette, and at his insistence, left him alone to say his prayers. Eventually, his life came to an end, but not before he told his companions that he thanked God for allowing him to perish doing the most fruitful work he could have ever prayed for and received, ministering to the Native Americans in the unsettled new world.

Marquette died on May 18, 1675. He was just shy of thirty-eight years old. He had spent over half his life, twenty-one years, in the Jesuit order. He had spent nine years in Canada.

The Unsolved Mysteries of Father Marquette's Many Graves

His companions buried him on a rise by the river and erected a simple cross, just as he had bravely and carefully described.

"The evening before his death, which was a Friday, he told them, very joyously, that it would take place on the morrow. He conversed with them during the whole day as to what would need to be done for his burial: about the manner in which they should inter him; of the spot that should be chosen for his grave; how his feet, his hands, and his face should be arranged; how they should erect a cross over his grave. He even went so far as to counsel them, three hours before he expired, that as soon as he was dead they should take the little hand bell of his chapel, and sound it while he was being put under ground. He spoke of all these things with so great tranquility and presence of mind that one might have supposed that he was concerned with the death and funeral of some other person, and not with his own."[106]

Largillier and Porteret were upset and Largillier had also been sick. Before leaving he took some dirt from Marquette's grave and rubbed it on his chest and felt immediate relief. The two were then able to continue on with the tasks Marquette had given them. They took a written copy of his confession to his Superior at Michilimackinac and relayed the story of the great priest's death.

After returning to Saint Ignace and reporting Marquette's passing with sadness, Largillier had another item of importance on his mind. He spoke with Father Henri Nouvel and asked to become a Brother of the Jesuit Order. He died in the service of the Jesuits at the Illinois mission in 1714.

Bones to Mackinac

"He always entreated God that he might end his life in these laborious missions, and that, like his dear St. Xavier, he might die in the midst of the woods, bereft of everything… "[107]

Marquette knew his requested assignment would be extremely difficult. Prior to his arrival in New France, several Jesuit priests and Jesuit lay brothers had been killed. There were many tragic examples. For instance, Father Isaac Jogues was captured by the Mohawks in 1646. He was tortured severely, and the ends of his fingers were chewed off, but he escaped. Eventually, he returned to the Mohawks, but was killed with a tomahawk. Jesuit Antoine Daniel was killed by the Iroquois then burned in his own church. Before being killed, parts of Father Jean Brebeuf's body were cut away and eaten as he watched. Jesuit Anne de Noue froze to death after losing his way during a blizzard. Other Jesuits were kidnapped or shot. Others simply disappeared.

Everyday life was hard. The French and Native Americans traveled on foot or in canoes. If a canoe capsized, the occupants could drown. Hypothermia might claim the lives of survivors of canoe wrecks or people who lost their way on foot. The Native Americans and French sometimes died from simple infections or the flu. They sometimes became lost, never to be found again. They sometimes were stalked by wolves or bear. Hunger was also a constant battle. Following is an account by Father Allouez describing a time when the population was battling hunger:

The Unsolved Mysteries of Father Marquette's Many Graves

"On a certain morning, a deer was found, dead since four or five days. It was a lucky acquisition for poor famished beings. I was offered some, and although the bad smell hindered some from eating it, hunger made me take my share. But I had in consequence an offensive odor in my mouth until the next day."[108]

Human contact could also be a great source of danger to the Jesuits. Though in many circumstances the Jesuits were loved by the people at their missions, there were notable exceptions. Some Jesuits were tortured and killed by those they sought to convert. The Native Americans questioned the Jesuits' loyalty when they ministered to enemy nations. The Native Americans noticed that European disease surfaced in their villages at the same time as the Jesuits. Some thought the Jesuits were witches due to their advanced abilities, such as, the ability to predict eclipses. At times, the Native Americans objected to the baptism of their children, believing that promises of the afterlife meant separation of the adults from the children. Disfavor spread when the priests did not recognize cultural taboos. For instance, some local tribes detested and feared the cross. Their enemies from the west, the Sioux, used crosses to put their warriors to death.

The Jesuits were trying to teach the Native Americans about God, a god with a magical and immense power, totally foreign to them. It was natural for them to fear what they couldn't understand. It was natural for them to resent a new religion and government that stripped them of their culture and freedoms and attempted to take away their free will, governance, and land.

Father Jacques Marquette must have had a particular way with people. Written accounts tell of the respect awarded him by not only the Huron, who had received instruction for decades prior to Marquette's arrival in New France, but also the Chippewa, and Illinois. The Sioux respected him enough

Bones to Mackinac

to make every attempt to abide by the peace treaty he helped to negotiate. Yet, the strongest showing of deep esteem and admiration came when the Odawa dug up his body and conveyed his bones to Saint Ignace.

Almost exactly two years after his death, a group of Odawa ventured to find the wooden cross marking his grave. They dug up Father Marquette's body, prepared his bones, and completed his trip to Michilimackinac.

It was typical for the Native Americans to live nomadic lives, living at villages like Saint Ignace and Sault Sainte Marie during summer months, and at traditional maple sugar places like Bois Blanc Island in the Straits of Mackinac or Sugar Island near Sault Sainte Marie in the spring. During the winter, they broke into smaller family groups and moved a distance from the rest. This was necessary as the game often became depleted at larger village sites.

Some of the Kiskakon Odawa had traveled south to carry out their winter hunt near Marquette's grave. On their return to Michilimackinac, they retrieved the good Father's bones.

As unusual as it may sound, perhaps due to their nomadic lifestyles, Native Americans would sometimes carry about their loved one's dead bodies or just their dried bones. There are accounts of families that carried deceased children with them for decades.

It was their practice to store such bodies on scaffolds high in the air, out of the reach of wolves, or in underground graves. Later, when tribes moved about the region, the bodies would be dug up or taken down from the scaffold. Using primitive tools like stone scrapers or their bare hands, they would strip the body of the flesh, leaving only the bones. It's likely the flesh was cremated in an open fire and left in the location of the preparation. The bones were dried, and sometimes dressed in cloth, painted, or packaged in a special backpack.

The Unsolved Mysteries of Father Marquette's Many Graves

When they retrieved Marquette from his original grave, they followed similar Native American customs. The quote that follows is from *Jesuit Relations*:

"They repaired, then, to the spot, and resolved among themselves to act in regard to the father as they are wont to do toward those for whom they profess great respect. Accordingly, they opened the grave, and uncovered the body; and, although the flesh and internal organs were all dried up, they found it entire, so that not even the skin was in any way injured. This did not prevent them from proceeding to dissect it, as is their custom. They cleansed the bones and exposed them to the sun to dry; then, carefully laying them in a box of birch bark, they set out to bring them to our Mission of Saint Ignace."[109]

On May 19, 1677, Marquette's body was retrieved from his Lower Peninsula grave. His bones were cleared of any remaining flesh in an act referred to as excarnation. His bones were scraped clean and likely the remaining flesh was cremated on site. Marquette's bones were disarticulated, meaning separated at the joints, and were placed in a specially prepared birch bark box. With great honor and respect, a funeral procession of near thirty canoes escorted Marquette's remains to Saint Ignace. The remains of his body again rode in the bottom of a canoe.

When the Odawa led party arrived in Saint Ignace, Father Superior Henri Nouvel and Father Phillipe Pierson, other Frenchmen, and Native Americans from different tribes met them on the beach. Father Nouvel questioned the party thoroughly, assuring they truly possessed the remains of the great priest. A few days later, Marquette's bones were humbly set to rest in the damp beach soils under the mission church of Saint Ignace de Michilimackinac.

Naming Taboo

Early Europeans wrote hundreds of passages regarding the Native American burial practices and death rites. While Christian burial practices and death rites remained relatively unchanged for hundreds of years, in fact, varying little throughout written history, Native American practices varied widely. From the 1600s to the 1800s, throughout Michigan and the Great Lakes region, dozens of variations on Native American body disposition were recorded. In most descriptions, bodies were placed under ground in the normal supine position that we would today expect, but examples have also been found of burials found standing straight up, sitting, or in fetal positions. Examples also exist where corpses were buried face down or folded in half at the waist and buried face down or face up.

In many descriptions, Native American dead weren't buried, but were suspended high in the air. Early Europeans came to Michigan's shores and found bodies sewn in animal skin bags and hung from trees or placed on scaffolds. In Lower Michigan, bodies of children were found tucked into tiny, carved-out living tree branches with wooden lids which fit the openings like box tops.

Odd occasions have been mentioned where corpses were never buried, nor suspended in the air, but were placed in caves, under rock ledges or rock piles, placed in hollow logs, or in one case in the Lower Peninsula, left propped in a primitive chair.

The Unsolved Mysteries of Father Marquette's Many Graves

Burials were sometimes placed in huge mass graves with hundreds of other bodies. Sometimes smaller mass interments were used resulting in wagon-wheel shaped circle patterns of burials. Sometimes the feet of all of the corpses pointed in. Sometimes the feet of all of the corpses pointed out.

On occasion, fields of small pits containing several burials each have been found. Bodies within such pit burials, or within the mass burials already discussed, were not always prepared for burial in the same manner as other bodies buried within the same pit. At times, these pit burials were cremated, or buried whole, or sometimes disarticulated like Marquette's skeleton.

Saint Ignace is arguably home to the largest concentration of seventeenth century cemeteries in the Midwest, and also, home to numerous unique Native American graves. More than a dozen different traditions have been recorded in the area. Saint Ignace also holds a unique place in history as the home of the second grave of the first European known to have died in Michigan, a grave which was uniquely based on both European and Native American burial traditions.

Jesuit Relations recorded the way Marquette's bones were scraped and broken apart at the joints prior to his second burial. This tale fascinated the European readers of *Jesuit Relations* and led to his lasting fame. Unfortunately, the exact locations of Marquette's graves weren't discussed in those texts. As a result, for over three hundred years people have searched for and debated the locations of Marquette's graves.

There are at least three locations in Michigan that have erected monuments and plaques claiming to be the site of Marquette's death. There are people who claim that the original burial place of Marquette was in Manistee, Michigan. Others claim it was in Frankfort, Michigan. Most people seem to believe the original burial place of Father Marquette is near Ludington, Michigan.

Naming Taboo

Though no one knows the answer for sure, Ludington has the distinction of being the location of the Pere Marquette River mouth. This river was named after Marquette and it seems more than obvious that it was named after the priest due to the fact that he died at the mouth. Within ten years of Marquette's death, maps were printed naming and showing the location of the Pere Marquette River. In addition, published accounts described the river and the grave site in the 1700s, 1800s, and 1900s.

Fifty years after Marquette left Saint Ignace, during travels through the Great Lakes in 1721, Father Pierre Charlevoix sought out the original grave. The territory was still wild and inhabited primarily by Native Americans and French fur traders. Charlevoix took great pains to identify the grave site. He questioned people. He commented that the Native Americans called the nearby river the River of the Black Gown and that the French had named it after Marquette. He said the fact that this was the river Marquette was buried beside was known by "constant tradition" and was affirmed by "some ancient missionaries".[110] He also visited Saint Ignace, remarking that the fort, likely the French fort, Fort de Buade, which was built after Marquette's death, and the residence of the missionaries were still standing. Many believe he didn't know that Saint Ignace was Marquette's final resting place during that time.

A hundred years later, American fur trader Gurdon Hubbard wrote that he visited the original burial place of Father Marquette. He said it was marked by a cross that stood next to the Marquette River. Hubbard is credited with the following words:

"Near the head of the Marquette River in the fall of 1818, I saw what was said to be the original cross of red cedar which marked where Marquette was buried. It was about three feet above the ground and leaning over. Our voyagers held it in

The Unsolved Mysteries of Father Marquette's Many Graves

veneration and were in the practice of resetting it when necessary. For several years after, I saw the cross when I passed the place."[111]

A few years after Gurdon Hubbard saw the cross, another priest, Father Gabriel Richard, visited the site and wrote that he had located the original grave. Father Richard was a priest assigned to the French and Native American missions in Michigan. Many of these missions were rooted in the work of the Jesuits in the 1600s. As part of his assignment, he visited the French and Native American villages at Michilimackinac and L'Arbre Croche, now known as Harbor Springs, Michigan.[112] When in 1821 he learned that the resident Odawa at L'Arbre Croche knew the location of Father Marquette's first burial site, he asked them to take him to it. His guides were descendants of the people that recovered and moved Father Marquette's bones to Saint Ignace. This tribal group once lived in Saint Ignace, but moved across the Straits of Mackinac around 1708.

Traveling by water as their Odawa ancestors had in 1677, he and his guides retraced the shore of Lake Michigan. He and the Odawa erected a new wooden cross in honor of the Jesuit.

A few years after Father Richard visited the original burial site, a lumber town called Pere Marquette sprung up along the river. An inhabitant of this town handed down this history about a man who worked in the village sometime between 1840 and 1882.

"… an old Frenchman who worked for Burr Caswell…was brought up at Mackinaw, and he used to relate to Mr. Caswell, how that, when a boy, he came with a boat's crew and a Catholic priest, and they put up a cross on the spot where they supposed Marquette to have been buried. The cross was erected on the bank of the channel near the bluff."[113]

Naming Taboo

Through the decades, the Ludington cross was replaced and upgraded several times. Several decades ago, a monument of substantial size was erected.

Frankfort, Michigan also has claimed to be the site of Marquette's death. Such claims seem to start in the year 1900, when officials from the Ann Arbor Railway found a skull and some bones while excavating for a hotel foundation.[114] For some reason, they declared that the remains were Marquette's skull and bones. Newspapers across America announced the find, ignoring the fact that the bones had been taken to Saint Ignace.

Claims that Manistee, a town only thirty minutes drive from Ludington, was Marquette's original resting place seem to be based on studies of ancient French maps. Manistee does have attributes similar to those described in the accounts of Father Marquette's death. There is a lake near the Lake Michigan shore. Maps from the 1600s and 1700s exist which could be used to support or refute this theory. Having said that, the "constant tradition" that Charlevoix described is not a clue to be overlooked. Oral history identifying a location can survive for centuries. One need only to look at a map of Michigan and read the French and Native American names to support this thinking.

Alas, like so many important historic sites, finding iron clad, positive proof of the location of the original grave site of Marquette is probably no longer likely. The removal of Marquette's bones from the first grave may have closed that door tightly. It's unfortunate. Though no longer the resting place for his bones, it's no less still a grave, as his flesh remained there.

The constant tradition that Charlevoix spoke of regarding the original grave was not kept regarding the location of Marquette's second grave. There seemed to be no local

79

tradition. Only vague recollections of the grave of some sort of important man survived and were passed from generation to generation.

While Saint Ignace had thrived in the 1600s, in the early 1700s the French soldiers left to found Detroit, Michigan. Most of the Huron and some of the Odawa moved to Detroit. Soon after, the Jesuits closed their mission in Saint Ignace and left. The population dropped to a handful of people.

Wars resulted in changes in governance. Speaking Native American and then French languages gave way to English. Oral history faded.

Complicating matters, when a person passed away, it was the custom of some tribes to refrain from using a deceased person's name. After death a man was referred to as "the great chief" and his name was not used unless it was given to another person in a process referred to as resuscitation (a ceremony in which a living person is given the name of a dead person, out of respect).

There are various old texts from throughout the region that discuss the burial and grave at Saint Ignace of an unnamed "great priest", "great missionary", or "the great bishop".

Saint Ignace Catholic Priest Edward Jacker wrote that while not identifying Marquette, local tradition held that a "bishop" was buried in Saint Ignace. He surmised that could mean the same as the Native American word, "Kitchimekatewikana-nie" which he translated to mean "great priest".

In another example, an account originated from Petoskey that stated that a "great priest" or Kitchi-ma-ka-da-na-co-na-yay died at the mouth of a river.[115]

Another book explained "Kitchimekatewikwanaie" means the great priest in Odawa and says that Cross Village was founded by the great priest.[116] There is a popular belief that missions founded among the Odawa on the northern shores of the Lower Peninsula date back to Marquette. L'Arbre Croche, which was said to stretch through the area between present day Cross Village, Michigan and Harbor Springs, Michigan, was likely the site of a satellite mission serviced by the Jesuits stationed at Saint Ignace.[117]

Despite this difficulty, by the mid to late 1800s, a number of curious people had found and began examining information about Father Marquette's graves. By the 200th anniversary of his death, hope had swelled in Saint Ignace that the second tomb of the first European man buried in Michigan might be found.

Rediscovery

In May of 1877, Saint Ignace was experiencing its first surge in population since the 1600s. Sawmills were being constructed along the bay. Merchants were building bakeries, stores, butcher shops, and hotels. Plans were underway for a railroad.

Peter D. Grondin was clearing an overgrown piece of property owned by Patrick Murray.[118] Murray was a well-to-do merchant who with his family owned about 600 acres of land in Saint Ignace. The parcel being cleared was at the rear of Murray's house near the present northwest corner of Marquette Street and North State Street. The Murrays had owned the property for over 25 years, but had never used the land that was being cleared. They had let it grow up to underbrush.

Grondin burned and cleared brush and cut down trees. Spruce, balsam, and juniper, a thick low lying evergreen brush, covered the site. As the clearing work progressed, a stone foundation was uncovered.

The foundation walls were two feet wide, a few inches tall, and formed a rectangle with the small side facing the lake. In the center of the foundation was a hole, ten feet by ten feet by five feet deep. It was assumed to be a cellar. Within this cellar, there was another, smaller hole which was about two feet deep. Connected to this building foundation on the west side was evidence of another, larger foundation with three compartments and fireplaces.

The Unsolved Mysteries of Father Marquette's Many Graves

Below David Murray, Patrick Murray's son, wrote in November of 1902 of the finding in 1877:

"In May 1877, my father, Patrick Murray, since deceased, was having cleared for garden purposes, ground near his home. The ground was covered with closely growing balsam, spruce, and juniper trees, such as cover the hills around the city today. When work had been completed, it exposed to view the foundation of a 36 x 40 building[119] with narrower part facing the lake. This foundation of flat limestone, such as would be used in lining up a log building, stood up so distinctly from the ground around that it could not [but] command attention."[120]

And from another source:

"There had been no building on this ground within memory of any living person; and trees that had stood there went to show that time had been long and the years many since any structure could have been there. My father, knowing from the history of this region that somewhere in Saint Ignace had stood the mission chapel of the Jesuits and in which Marquette had been laid when brought here from the east shore of Lake Michigan, by the Indians, in 1677, and further, the traditions among old French and Indians pointing to the head of the bay as the place where, as they said, a great bishop was buried... "[121]

Examination of the site produced evidence of early Frenchmen, and of the Catholic religion, such as Jesuit rings, beads, a small lock, and crucifixes. They also found fragments of worked metal including copper and iron. The Jesuits manufactured metal items in primitive blacksmiths' shops, and gave those items to their faithful. They bartered repair work for goods and services and traded away or used some items. It was assumed that these metal artifacts proved the location was accurate.

Rediscovery

Father Edward Jacker was called to the site. Jacker, a Catholic priest who served at Saint Ignace and Mackinac Island in the late 1800s, studied history, in particular, the history of early Catholic missions. Jacker had extensively studied the history of Father Marquette and probably felt a kinship with Marquette. Like Marquette, Jacker often expressed a desire to serve Native American populations. Also, just as Marquette had, he started his work in the Great Lakes region at Sault Sainte Marie. Also similar to Marquette, Jacker spoke several languages including his native German, English, and several Native American languages or dialects. Jacker took a leadership role in the search of the site.

When further digging revealed pieces of birch bark and fragments of bone, it was assumed Marquette's tomb was rediscovered. Mr. Murray then had second thoughts. He felt it was improper to allow random rifling of the grave of such an important and beloved missionary. He was also in disagreement with Father Jacker as to the disposition of any artifacts. They also disagreed about what should happen to Father Marquette's bones. Mr. Murray put a halt to the excavation. In the following quote, "the point" refers to Point Saint Ignace.

"The priest believes the location to be the correct one, and is anxious to excavate, but Mr. Murray refuses to permit it without a pledge that whatever is found shall not be carried away from the point. He offers to give the ground for the erection of a church or monument on the spot. But insists that the sacred relics, if found, must be left where they have for two centuries rested.[122]

Murray forbid digging for several months.

The months which Mr. Murray prohibited digging gave Father Jacker time for research. He contacted prominent historians and obtained additional research material. Father

The Unsolved Mysteries of Father Marquette's Many Graves

Jacker spoke several languages and had the records of the Catholic Church at his disposal. Early French maps were secured and experts in colonial history traveled to Saint Ignace to offer theories. The more they learned, the more experts agreed with the early assessments.

During this period, rumors circulated that Marquette was buried with treasure. Residents of the area continued to search for and collect artifacts despite the ban. The finds included jewelry and crucifixes, and area residents, including the Murray family, collected several prime items.[123]

Several months passed. The Catholic Church approached the Murray family and requested the official digging be allowed to continue. Murray acquiesced in September. Digging again commenced, and as the description below details, more possible evidence was found.

"The bottom of the ancient cellar was found covered to the height of about a foot with a decayed vegetable matter. At one corner, a post superficially burned and partly decayed was still standing in its original (perpendicular) position; it was embedded in sand and gravel, in consequence of caving in the side of the cellar. Underneath the vegetable soil, on the ancient floor, lay scattered pieces of small timber, more or less charred and decayed; lumps of mortar, showing the impress of cedar logs; wrought nails and spikes; a door-hinge; fragments of large glass jar and small pieces of colored glass. Toward the west end of the cellar, some small pieces of charred birch bark were found, and it soon became evident that here a small excavation had once been made in the bottom of the cellar, to a depth of about two feet. This space contained, besides sand blackened by a mixture of charcoal, many small particles of pure lime; a large amount of birch bark in shreds, generally crisp and partially charred, and two small fragments of bone. At the bottom of this smaller excavation lay a large pieces of strong birch bark, in a horizontal position, and supported by three almost decayed sticks."[124]

The digging continued to a depth of two to three feet throughout the body of the foundation. Finding nothing in the main part of the structure, the digging focused on the cellar area. There they found a burned, decayed post, a piece of paper, nails, a hinge, burned hewn planks and joists, a piece of glass from a bottle or jar, fragments of a saw, fish spears, pieces of gun locks, a chisel, screws, mortar, lime, bark, a sliver of mirror, a piece of flat birch bark supported by three sticks, and two suspected pieces of bone.

Digging continued with or without the presence of Father Jacker or Mr. Murray.[125] Tourists dug. Children dug. Shovelfuls of dirt were cast about without order. People sifted through spoils.

While searching through loose sand within the excavated area, a man named Joseph Marley found thirty-six[126] fragments of bone. He took his collection of bones to Father Jacker, who already possessed what he described as two "doubtful" bone fragments. Later, a presumed skull fragment was also found. Said Jacker of Marley's find:

"The result of his search was of such a character that he considered himself obliged to put me in possession of it. What was my astonishment when he displayed on my table a number of small fragments of bones, in size from an inch in length down to a mere scale, being in all thirty-six, and to all appearances, human. Being alone, after nightfall, I washed the bones."[127]

Jacker took the bone fragments to a surgeon from Cheboygan, Michigan. This surgeon was identified only by the last name Pommier in Jacker's correspondence. The surgeon told Jacker the bones were human.[128]

Arguments For and Against

The bones of saintly Father Marquette were declared found, but there were still many unanswered questions. Why were there so few bones? Were the bones really human? Why weren't the bones in the birch bark box? Father Jacker's circumstantial evidence was ample. He had the support of experts, written records, and more than a half dozen maps from the 1600s.

Jacker's maps and other written evidence indicated that in the 1600s, the chapel and grave were located at the head of East Moran Bay in what is now the City of Saint Ignace. This relatively level area is surrounded by hills. Those hills helped limit the possible locations. The discovered site was within the appropriate area.

According to the maps, the Jesuit compound was north of a group of cabins belonging to French traders. In a newspaper account from the late 1800s, Jacker pointed out they had found the suspected remains of the French cabins southeast of the presumed grave site. There they found seven or eight[129] small foundations with cellars and remnants of chimneys. In the soil around these foundations they found fragments of lime, a building material which would have been used by the French villagers.[130]

Maps from the 1600s showed the Jesuit chapel was surrounded by a fort. That fort was located south of another, larger fort, which surrounded a Huron village. North of the

The Unsolved Mysteries of Father Marquette's Many Graves

presumed grave site, Jacker found evidence of a fort wall. He assumed it was the Huron fort.

Jacker was right about the fort wall. One hundred years later, archaeologists confirmed the remains of a fort wall just north of the site of the discovered foundation which archaeologists had named "the Marquette Mission site". Within the identified Huron fort, archaeologists found the remains of long houses, traditional Huron housing, confirming that the fort was a Native American fort rather than the Jesuit fort. It couldn't be the French military fort known to have existed at Saint Ignace, Fort de Buade, as that fort had a triple wall of stakes.

Further, the general shape, layout, and size of the presumed mission foundation were taken as positive evidence. In 1688, French military officer Louis Armand de Lom d'Arce, Baron de Lahontan, the French authority responsible for some of the most detailed early maps of the area, described the mission as being two different but connected buildings. He said, "In this place the Jesuits have a little house, or college, adjoining to a sort of a church, and enclosed with pales that separate it from the village of the Huron."[131]

Jacker also relied on the artifacts found at the site as evidence. The Native Americans built using bent poles and bark. The French built log structures. The artifacts found indicated the buildings that once existed on the site of the foundation were log. The remnants of lime, forged metal, and nails made it likely they had found the remains of French buildings.

Other evidence relied upon by Jacker was not as strong. A great deal of weight was placed on the fact that there were no chimney remains within the eastern part of the foundation, but there were chimney or fire pit remains in the adjacent building. Jacker took this as evidence that that structure had been a church with an attached living quarters. He did not

Arguments For and Against

consider that in the 1600s, the village would have included many buildings without chimneys such as storage buildings, ice houses, and fur warehouses.

Another point people questioned had to do with the birch bark coffin. Jacker had concluded that birch bark was an important clue, stating he believed that the bones were interred in the flotilla's birch bark box. No written evidence found states the birch bark box became Marquette's resting place. In fact, there is no description of Marquette's coffin. Birch bark would have been an extremely common material in a Native American community. It would have been used in cooking, house building, canoe building, and to construct containers for storage. Bark in the soil didn't specifically point to a disintegrated birch bark coffin. Further, the Jesuits had skilled staff, donné, and Brothers, who were metal workers and builders. The Jesuits at Saint Ignace had access to sawn lumber. The Jesuits tended to turn toward European traditions when the choice arose. A coffin made of sawn planks seems like an idea the Jesuits would have turned toward.

The charred building material found at the site was also suggested to be evidence that the former mission church had been found. Historians commonly believe that prior to abandoning the mission in the early 1700s, the Jesuits burned their own chapel to prevent looting; however, charred material would be a common finding in the soil around a seventeenth century village. Fire was a greatly feared hazard in the 1600s. There are records of whole villages burning due to careless smoking, warfare, or accidental fires.

Those interested wondered, if the Jesuits had burned the chapel around 1705, why they hadn't first removed Marquette's bones? To some, leaving the precious bones of Marquette behind when the mission was burned seemed counter-intuitive, particularly when the proposed reason for burning the mission was to protect the mission from

The Unsolved Mysteries of Father Marquette's Many Graves

desecration. Author Samuel Hedges, who was present during part of the digging,[132] made the following point:

"They would not have left the remains of a saint to desecration any more than he would have left the sacred vessels of the altar to desecration. There are no documentary evidences that the Fathers of the mission destroyed the church, just as there are no documentary evidences that when the mission was abandoned Marquette's remains were left where they had been buried."[133]

Hedges went further, "The ease with which his sacred remains might have been removed, again leads us to doubt that the Fathers destroyed the church without having taken them away... The skeleton was not intact. The bones had been [taken] apart by the Indians when they prepared them for transportation from the shore of Lake Michigan."[134]

That is an interesting argument, but if Marquette's bones had been removed by the Jesuits, it would have been done with a great deal of ceremony. Take for example written accounts describing how the bones of Jesuit martyr Father Jean Brebeuf were handled after he was tortured and killed in an Iroquois attack in Huronia in 1649. His body was disinterred and removed, first to Quebec, and then back to Midland, Ontario to the Church of the Martyrs. Initially, Brebeuf was buried in a wooden coffin with a two inch by four inch lead plaque identifying him. He was later dug up, his flesh was removed, then the bones were scraped and boiled in lye. The lye and flesh was thought returned to the coffin. The bones were dried in an oven, wrapped in silk, put into a specially built chest, then sent to Quebec. Later they were returned to Midland, Ontario. His skull was placed in a silver reliquary, a container built for human remains, and is now on display in the Martyrs' Shrine in Midland, Ontario along with the bones and skulls of several Jesuits from the 1600s.

Arguments For and Against

A great deal of thought was put to the question of leaving or taking Marquette's bones. A great deal of thought was put to the question of burning or not burning the chapel. One historian proposed the theory that the Jesuits did not purposely burn the mission, that perhaps they abandoned the mission, planning to return sometime later, only to find it had burned. Another theory presented was that the mission was burned in a hostile situation, an attack, and by the time the hostilities abated, the location of the grave was lost. They thought perhaps it had been burned by hostile agents or by accident. Without the chapel to act as a grave marker, maybe the Jesuits couldn't find the bones.

The missionary Pierre Francois Xavier Charlevoix stated that the missionary quarters at Saint Ignace were still standing in 1721.[135] Given that the living quarters were connected and were still standing for more than a decade after the mission was abandoned, it's hard to imagine that Marquette's second grave couldn't be found, even after the hypothetical burning of the chapel.

Doubters pressed Jacker as to why so few bones were found. Marquette's skeleton would have likely initially included fifteen to twenty pounds of bones, live weight, with around two hundred bones total. A dozen of those bones would have been more than a foot long. Merely a couple of ounces of bones had been found in total in 1877. Jacker proposed that the missing bones could have been stolen centuries before by people who coveted any powers or magic the bones might hold.[136]

As unlikely as this may sound, this could be plausible. Body parts and human bones were once treated much differently than today, and it was possible that the bones were considered to hold great power. There are accounts of Catholic officials taking the bones of Jesuits and making potions of them. One passage in *Jesuit Relations*, says that a tea[137] with healing powers was made of the bones of one Jesuit.

The Unsolved Mysteries of Father Marquette's Many Graves

Author Samuel Hedges was skeptical about this, too. He didn't believe in the theory that the grave was looted and the bones stolen. As to the questions which arose regarding the relatively small number of bones, Hedges provided this important insight:

"Per conversations with some of those who were present at the time the search was made and who took part in it, we are constrained to believe that whatever separation of the remains there was was due to the manner in which the excavating was done. Too many had part in it and there was not a systematic uncovering of the entire church site. Digging was done here and there. The result was what might have been expected; confusion and disorder in the work... Digging was going on all the time. Even children were engaged in poking about the dirt with sticks."[138]

Whether entire skeletons or small bone fragments, human bones aren't found just anywhere. Finally and perhaps most importantly, upon hearing the story of Marquette's Saint Ignace burial, many people countered the doubters by questioning how the bones could be anyone but Marquette.

Saint Ignace is an unusual place. Buried beneath it are uncountable remains, prepared for burial in uncountable, unusual ways. Within a stone's throw of the purported mission site and in every direction are numerous unmarked graves. For instance, at the time of the rediscovery of Marquette's bones, Murray mentioned that these weren't the first human remains they had found on the property. Prior to the finding of the foundation, they had discovered a post-contact burial in front of the foundation. Just across the yard to the north eight burials dating from 170 A. D. were found in 1973. Three burials in wooden coffins were discovered around two hundred feet south of the foundation. To the north of Marquette's purported burial site, around the next intersection, were found several pit burials and two corpses

Arguments For and Against

buried standing straight up. Another burial, suspected to have been female, was found under the roadway east of the purported mission site. More remains were found just north of Reagan Street behind a more modern church which has since been torn down. Further, a statement in the book *Before the Bridge* discussed "multiple bodies" found in 1936 on Marquette Street, the street south of the Museum of Ojibwa Culture and Father Marquette Mission Park. Two of those corpses were chained together, perhaps indicating that these were Huron burials, as the Huron chained murderers to their victims as a form of punishment. With all of the unmarked graves within a few blocks, and with the potential for many more, does the existence of bone fragments at the site become a less significant clue?

Supporting Oral History Leads to More Questions

As the dig generated excitement in the community, Jacker strove to gather more information to support the conclusion that they had found Marquette's second grave. Some older folks added some thought provoking oral history to Jacker's written history and maps. They told Jacker that Native American elders had long been seen stopping to say prayers near the site.

After Marquette's death, when Jesuits still occupied the Saint Ignace area, they had instructed parishioners to say prayers at the grave of Marquette. The following passage from *Jesuit Relations* was likely written just after Marquette's death.

"The [Native Americans] often come to pray over his tomb. Not to mention more than this instance, a young girl, aged nineteen or twenty years, whom the late father had instructed, and who had been baptized in the past year, fell sick, and applied to Father Nouvel to be bled and to take certain remedies. The Father prescribed to her, as sole medicine, to come for three days and say a pater and three aves at the tomb of Father Marquette. She did so, and before the third day was cured, without bleeding or any other remedies."[139]

Could this tradition have lasted for 200 years?

It also came to Jacker's attention that townspeople remembered that a black cross once stood near the site of the

The Unsolved Mysteries of Father Marquette's Many Graves

foundation, more specifically, "on or near the beach."[140] As with the cedar cross that had been planted at Marquette's original grave site, a black cross could have marked Marquette's second grave. He considered it may have marked several things of importance. Jacker knew it might also have been a marker indicating the site of the mission. He considered that it also could have marked a lost, centuries-old Catholic cemetery.

Any of the possible uses of the black cross would add to Jacker's circumstantial evidence and ultimately led Jacker to think about the importance of finding a Catholic cemetery. It could further the understanding of how the village was laid out and support his theories about Marquette's gravesite. Father Jacker wondered about the likelihood of a Catholic cemetery adjacent to the mission in a letter to Reverend Father Chrysostom Verwyst. In this quoted passage, he revealed that there was other surprising evidence of a Catholic cemetery:

"In digging a cellar (in front of what we now believe to have been the Jesuits' church), Mr. David Murray, Sr., had even struck a grave once occupied, to judge from the silken stuffs and gold borders found in it, by some person of distinction. Here then in front of the church, as once was customary, the cemetery would seem to have been located."[141] [142]

It is logical that the mission had a cemetery, but there is no written record of one near the head of the bay in downtown Saint Ignace.[143] The 1600s was a time of war, disease, and sometimes starvation. Infant mortality was extremely high. Death rates in general were high. The Jesuits had a presence at Saint Ignace for thirty-five years. The Jesuits must have had Christian dead to bury in addition to Father Marquette.

The Jesuits would not have favored burial of their parishioners in Native American cemeteries, in fact, there are recorded instances where the Jesuits went to great lengths to

Supporting Oral History Leads to More Questions

prevent burial of the Native American Catholics and Frenchmen outside of Catholic cemeteries. Jesuits throughout North America commented that parishioners in fear of dying from illness would go through great efforts to die near their clergy, chapels, and Catholic cemeteries, in order to assure they would be properly buried.[144] The Jesuits even went so far as to gather the severed limbs of torture victims and transport them to Catholic cemeteries. Catholic clergy strictly buried their dead in Catholic cemeteries or under their churches.

It would have been likely the Jesuits had a church-yard graveyard for the Christians in the 1600s. The French Catholics buried their dead in consecrated ground, specifically defined and blessed by clergy. Within properly prepared Catholic grave-yards, steps could be taken to banish evil spirits and the devil. Those deemed unfit to be buried with the pious dead such as suicide victims, murderers, unbaptized infants and adults, and the mentally ill could be excluded. Fences were erected to keep out animals. It would have been likely to be a site near the Jesuit fort, or even within the Jesuit fort, so the Jesuits could make sure it was respected. Bodies were prepared for the Resurrection with heads to the west and feet to the east.

As this book has previously discussed, many unmarked graves have been found in the area around the Marquette Mission site. Very few of those have characteristics matching Christian burials, but there are some. An old, hand-drawn map was recently discovered in the archives of the Michilimackinac Historical Society showing three burials in coffins around two hundred feet south of the Marquette Mission site. The unidentified author relates that the burials were found in coffins buried in relative alignment. The map stated the heads of all three burials were in the west end of the coffins. One was six to eight feet from the sidewalk on

99

The Unsolved Mysteries of
Father Marquette's Many Graves

the west right of way of North State Street, the main street in town. The other two were found slightly north of the first, on the east side of an alley which parallels North State Street. The author of this map stated the burials on the alley were four feet deep and in lumber boxes. These are typical aspects of Christian burials. Though these graves cannot be Marquette, they could be Christian burials from the 1600s.

As Jacker realized, finding such a cemetery could lead to more information about the layout of the Jesuit compound. Catholic dead were often buried in cemeteries along the church walls. Also, Catholics buried parishioners under their churches. It's possible there were burials other than Marquette underneath the floor of the church at the Marquette Mission. The church in the fort in Mackinaw City (built circa 1743) had evidence of a cemetery to the east of the church. Burials were found outside and inside of the church foundation in Mackinaw City. Burials also existed under the Catholic Church on Mackinac Island and under the church in Harbor Springs. Burials such as the burial with silk and gold and the three burials in board boxes might help delineate the layout of the mission and help to prove or disprove Jacker's theories.

The oral history regarding the black cross and the elders praying on site pointed to the fact that they had found the right location. Circumstantial evidence piled up. Yet, there still remained a lack of specific, indisputable proof. Father Jacker worried that he was accepting mere coincidences as fact. Did Father Jacker wish to find the grave so badly he was willing to shrug off things that didn't add up? Below, he wrote another historian about his doubts:

"So long I had wished—and I candidly confess it, even prayed—for the discovery of Father Marquette's grave, and now that so many evidences concurred to establish the fact of having been on the spot where we hoped to find it, I felt reluctant to believe it."[145]

Supporting Oral History Leads to More Questions

Jacker seemed conflicted, sometimes stiffly supporting his conclusions, sometimes waffling. Below he wrote historian and leading expert on early Catholic history in America, John Gilmary Shea:

"Everything it seems to me, answers the requirements of good circumstantial proof... but if you or any one else are leaning more on the side of doubt, I shall not quarrel with you."[146]

And below, still unable to fully and completely trust his findings, Jacker expressed his opinion in a letter he wrote Reverend Father Chrysostom Verwyst from his assignment at Eagle Harbor, Michigan on May 4, 1886:

"Is it then, you may ask, absolutely certain that the modest monument erected by the people of the neighborhood, in the City of Saint Ignace, marks the true site of Father Marquette's grave? I am not yet prepared to say so. But I have not heard of, nor can I imagine, any circumstance connected with our search, that would warrant any positive doubt."[147]

Other historians offered doubts. In a paper read before the Chicago Historical Society, Henry Higgins Hurlbut called the findings a sheer delusion, a fraud, and a fiction.[148] In a softer assessment, J. Holzknecht said:

"... it can hardly be said that we have the body or bones of Pere Marquette. What we have however is certainly valuable, especially if it could ever be proved beyond a doubt that they are the remains of Father Marquette, which could be done only by miracles."[149]

Convinced that the grave of Marquette had been found, the people of Saint Ignace erected a monument on the site of the foundation in 1882 under the supervision of Reverend Kilian Haas. Edward Jacker was no longer the parish priest at Saint Ignace. He was reassigned to Marquette, Michigan in 1880.

What Happened to the Bones

Jacker and the townspeople of Saint Ignace differed in their level of certainty about the grave site. There was another thing they disagreed about; what should happen to the bones? The new parish priest, Father Kilian Haas, pressured Jacker to send him the bone fragments found during the digging. Jacker had other plans.

Two letters written by Father Edward Jacker to Reverend Father Lalumiere, S. J. are published in *The Grave and Relics of Father Marquette* by Reverend H. S. Spalding. The first was written in Hancock, Michigan on August 15, 1882. In it Jacker said:

"When my successor, Father Kilian, insisted on my delivering up to him what I possessed of Father Marquette's reputed remains, I sent him about one fourth of the fragments of bone, together with a small selection from the diverse articles, pieces of evidence, as we might call them, found in the cellar and in the grave. Will your Reverence please let me know whether the Rev. Father Rector and the faculty of your college are willing to receive my collection… ?"[150]

And then 10 days later Jacker wrote:

"Here are all the bones left in my hands, after sending about seven similar fragments to Father Kilian of Saint Ignace. The other articles - pieces of bark, wood, iron, etc., I shall either send or bring to you in a short time."[151]

The Unsolved Mysteries of Father Marquette's Many Graves

Seven fragments of bone were sent to Reverend Kilian Haas. He solicited funds for the monument which was constructed on the Murray property, and buried those seven bones, and an assortment of artifacts from the site, under the monument.

Jacker didn't approve of reburying the bones and artifacts. As such, he arranged to send what was reported to be nineteen bone fragments to Marquette University in Milwaukee, Wisconsin along with burned wood, bark, and other unidentified artifacts.[152] Father Edward Jacker explained:

"Some of the remains were re-interred under the monument together with specimens of the debris. Other pieces are in the possession of a number of admirers of Father Marquette, all over the country. The greatest and most interesting collection (the bones being arranged in a neat casket, presented for that purpose, by Reverend Father Faeber of St. Louis), will be preserved in the Marquette College of Milwaukee. I thought it would be safer."[153]

The total number of bone fragments and bones found was reported in numerous places to be between thirty-five and thirty-nine. Jacker stated it was thirty-five, thirty-six, thirty-seven, and thirty-nine pieces of bone in different texts.

Several bone fragments were given away as souvenirs, never to be seen or heard of again. In a paper written by Father Francis Shulak, a friend of Father Jacker, he stated that he kept a small bone given to him by Jacker in his vest pocket.[154]

Seven bones were buried under the monument which still stands on the Marquette Mission site.

Bone fragments with a total weight of less than one ounce were sent to Marquette University in Milwaukee, Wisconsin where they were kept in the Archives Department of Special Collections. Those fragments were at Marquette University from 1882 until 2022. They were stored away.

What Happened to the Bones

In 2014, University Archivist, Michelle Sweetser, from Marquette University confirmed that the bone fragments were there. The collection was housed in fifteen small white boxes with red wax seals which were kept in a larger wooden box, specially designed to store them. Ms. Sweetsyer said that one or two of the boxes were opened in 1984 when the university allowed the bone fragments to be X-rayed. She explained, "the tests seems to have indicated they were human."

Ms. Sweetsyer knew of no other testing. She explained that any testing which might involve invasive techniques wasn't allowed by the university. As the likely remains of a sacred individual, the bones were treated with careful respect.

Though some of the artifacts found were also shipped to Marquette University, others were buried under the monument. Still others were said to have been kept and used as display items in local museums. Miscellaneous dug up items were removed and shipped to unknown places including pieces of birch bark that might now be used for carbon dating. At least one piece of presumed coffin (birch bark) was sent to a Catholic church that stood at a portage Marquette and Joliet had used in Wisconsin. That church has since been abandoned and it's unclear what happened to this important artifact.[155]

The Murrays eventually divided the parcel of land where the foundation was found. The eastern most portion was sold to a man named Siegfried Highstone.[156] He built an opera house on the site. The area where the foundation was found became a park, and eventually, a National Historic Landmark.

"The family gave the hallowed ground which contained the grave to the Detroit Jesuits, who marked off a plot 40 feet square and erected a tablet and inscriptions telling of the grave. The portion of the lot remaining before this square was sold to S. Highstone, who there operated an opera house.

The Unsolved Mysteries of Father Marquette's Many Graves

Later the City of Saint Ignace purchased the area from Mr. Highstone and the entire plot has been made a park. At the rear of the park stands the Murray homestead, the same which was established well over an half-century ago."[157]

Time passed and members of the Murray family passed away. Several Murray family obituaries emphasized their part in the finding. Mrs. Mary Jane Murray's obituary, cited above, mentions finding Father Marquette's grave three times.

Modern Findings

In 1675, the French had only begun to explore North America. Among those early brave souls, less than a hundred had reached the shores of the Great Lakes. Among those were several whose objective was not potential riches or fame, but the conversion of the Native Americans to Catholicism. Among those was a stand out, Jacques Marquette. He was loved by many and admired by many more. Unfortunately, he was destined to become the first European to die on Michigan's soil.

Beginning after the discovery of the foundation on the Murray parcel in 1877, and continuing today, Marquette's life and Marquette's graves have been favorite subjects of debate for historians, clergy, and archaeologists.

After the purported rediscovery of the grave site, Father Jacker gave interviews to newspapers, spoke at conferences, and published articles on the findings. He and the discoveries became the subject of many papers and publications. Interested parties researched and read. A vast number of books were soon published discussing Marquette's ministry and explorations and debating the location of his graves.

The site of the Marquette mission was home to Jesuits, French soldiers, fur traders, the Huron, and the Odawa for over thirty years. With its rich history and mix of different cultures, the Marquette Mission site became an interest of archaeologists and historians. Beginning around 1970, several archaeological excavations took place.

The Unsolved Mysteries of Father Marquette's Many Graves

The first professional team to excavate the Marquette Mission site began work in the summer of 1971. During the dig, they found artifacts and evidence of seventeenth century buildings, as well as evidence of a prehistoric Native American occupation. After digging at the Marquette Mission site, a report was produced stating no conclusive evidence of the mission had been found.

In 1972, the seven presumed Marquette bone fragments put under the monument by Reverend Kilian Haas in 1882 were retrieved and tested by archaeologists. According to an article published in the Detroit News in 1985, the testing found the seven fragments were bird and animal bones and part of a cow's skull.[158] The testing did not find any human remains.

In the 1980s, archaeologists conducted excavations spanning several years in the immediate area surrounding the Marquette Mission site. Archaeologists discovered thousands of artifacts, large and small, and evidence that helped to piece together a picture of life in the seventeenth century village of Michilimackinac. Archaeologists formed theories, embraced opinions, and made claims of interest. Opinions were offered that Fort de Buade was built on the water, south of the identified Marquette Mission site; however, archaeologists had not found the remains of a fort that had Fort de Buade's described triple wall. Digs proved that the fort walls of the Huron fort and first Odawa fort stretched under North State Street and were built very near the shore of Lake Huron. Digging proved that the north boundary of the seventeenth century occupation ended at a stream that had once existed near Reagan Street. It was discovered that the forts and other seventeenth century structures were torn down several times, redesigned, and reconstructed. The remains of long-houses, typical Native American housing, were found within the located forts. Those long-houses were aligned north to south.

Modern Findings

Extensive notes on the 1980s digs are housed at Lake Superior State University. There are hundreds of pages of notes on file regarding the Marquette Mission site, many of which originate from Dr. Susan Schacher. Dr. Susan Schacher was contracted by the Downtown Development Authority of the City of Saint Ignace during the 1980s. She wrote archaeological reports on sites downtown in 1983, 1984, 1985, and 1986. She published findings in the book, *Calumet and Fleur-de-Lys*, and in other publications. In those papers, archaeologists were mentioned who did believe the digs had revealed the site of the mission chapel. Most of the located professional opinions did not concur. In a letter to a fellow researcher, a few years before her death in 2007, Dr. Schacher said the phrase "the Marquette Mission site" was a misnomer as no evidence of the mission had ever been found.[159] Other professionals published opinions in journals and reports agreeing. Recently, during his testimony regarding the impact of the Line 5 tunnel on the Straits of Mackinac, respected archaeologist Dr. Charles Cleland stated the following regarding the purported Marquette Mission site, "Although the Museum at Michigan State University has conducted extensive excavations at this site, there is much of the site area that has not been explored. The burial site of Father Marquette is thought to be somewhere on the unexcavated portion."[160]

Believe or disbelieve? Archaeologists painted a grim picture. Though a few statements have surfaced indicating a belief that the mission site had been found, most concurred that it was not. And the efforts to find the site were broad in scope, stretching many years, and in multiple locations. Teams of learned people were involved.

Yet, there is one more mystery, one more inconsistency, that could mean the location of the Marquette Mission site and Marquette's bones are as claimed. It seems that in 1877, the location of the stone foundation was not thoroughly

The Unsolved Mysteries of Father Marquette's Many Graves

documented. By the time archaeologists began to explore the site a hundred years later, it was no longer clear exactly where the foundation and cellar were. Archaeologists discovered the stone markers installed as part of the monument which were meant to mark the outlines of the foundation had not been placed correctly.[161] They used the handwritten notes of Father Jacker and tried to relocate the exact placement of foundation and cellar.

When archaeologists did find the original site, or what they thought was the site, they discovered that an outhouse had been built on the immediate edge of the chapel site in 1879, two years after the foundation was found and just prior to the installation of the monument. They also made statements in different texts that said the trenches and pits left from the digging in 1877 had been backfilled with trash originating from the adjacent Highstone opera house property.[162] That's odd. Did someone knowingly construct an outhouse on a sacred, historic site, the burial site of a precious individual. Before placing the monument did they fill the dig site with garbage? It all sounds unlikely.

Unfortunately, modern study has not fully resolved lingering questions. Like Jacker, a reader could reasonably support their opinion with overwhelmingly convincing circumstantial evidence, but would have to admit to having no iron-clad proof.

It does have to be stated that Jacker's theories as to the layout of the town do square remarkably with what we now know is true. Marquette's grave could be no further north than the currently identified Marquette Mission site due to the known location of the Huron fort. Lake Huron lies to the east. To the west is a bluff which curves in a C shape, wrapping around the level ground where the French, Huron, and Odawa were known to live. The remaining level area south of the Marquette Mission site measures only about 1,000 feet by

Modern Findings

1,000 feet. This area is only ten to fifteen acres in size. Located within the identified ten to fifteen acres in the 1600s were the structures belonging to the Jesuits, the French fur traders, and soldiers. Occupying the northern part of this space was the Jesuit fort which enclosed the chapel and Jesuit living quarters. The French village, and perhaps Fort de Buade, occupied the southern part of this space. If the currently identified mission site and Marquette's grave are not correct, the clues available leave no doubt that it is within a mere few hundred feet.

Luckily for most, the exact location of the grave is less important than knowing the general location. For those insisting on knowing more, Francis Borgia Steck, an ardent researcher of Marquette's history once said, "History is and will always remain a progressive science."[163]

Marquette's Legacy

There are thousands of documents discussing Marquette's life and legacy. Some authors present biased information, sometimes inflating and sometimes ignoring Marquette's accomplishments.

Certain authors push hard to minimize Louis Joliet's contributions to the trip down the Mississippi, suggesting that Marquette was the navigator, team leader, or mastermind. Though only in his late 20s, Joliet was a great and experienced explorer, quite capable of leading the excursion, and proved it was so by leading two trips to Hudson's Bay after his trip with Marquette to explore the Mississippi River. We may never know if Marquette was an equal to Joliet, the leader of the Mississippi trip, or if his contribution was confined to that of a religious representative. Just being a part of such an important expedition, acting peacefully along the way, and providing written accounts of the trip, makes Marquette hugely important to North American history.

Various locations lay claim to having been places where Marquette resided, the site of his burial, or even simply a place he once stopped for the night. Some associations with Marquette are plausible; some are much less so.

Marquette is often credited with founding Sault Sainte Marie, Saint Ignace, and Chicago. Though many texts label Marquette as the founder of various places, he isn't really. In Saint Ignace, for instance, the oldest Native American burials

The Unsolved Mysteries of Father Marquette's Many Graves

date to thousands of years prior to the arrival of the French. He was likely not even the first European to reside in or visit those locations. If he was one of the first Europeans to arrive at these places, he was not alone, as he traveled with other priests, servants, and slaves.

He does deserve credit for his positive and loving approach to what was, for some, the first contact between the Native Americans and the Europeans. He seems to have treated the Native Americans with respect, and seemed to relish interaction with these new cultures. He opened his eyes to the wonder around him. He didn't complain of the difficulties of missionary work. He didn't focus on unmet goals or put an emphasis only on that which he felt should be eradicated from the Native American lifestyle. He did not follow the example of some missionaries who sought to tame the Native Americans, seeking a subservient result. Marquette seemed to step back and more carefully consider how to blend the existing Native American cultural practices with French Christian practices.

Marquette used his station to preach civility and advocate peace between the Native American tribes. According to his admittedly biased French chroniclers, he was instrumental in arranging temporary peace between the dispersed tribes and the Sioux tribes, despite the fact that they had warred for decades. He discouraged the cycle of revenge attacks. He nursed the sick, and there would have been many, as the death rates were disturbing in Marquette's time.

It's not well known that he produced some of the first written records describing flora, fauna, and geography originating from the central areas of the North American continent. He wrote of the remarkable life of the Native American tribes of North America. He wrote some of the first written records regarding Michigan, the Midwest, and of course, the Mississippi River.

Marquette's Legacy

Other Jesuits listed Marquette's traits to include joy, gentleness, encouragement, patience, devotion, endurance, and great zeal. We can also gather that he was a brave man. We can gather that he was a strong man. His grasp of languages would lead us to believe he must have been an intelligent man. Ironically, maybe one of the most notable attributes that Marquette possessed was remarkable humility. Marquette wanted to die in the forest with no possessions. He had requested only a simple, wooden cross to mark his grave. Instead, uncountable monuments have been built on his behalf. There is no end to the number of books that have been written about him. His name has been applied to towns, counties, rivers, and a railroad. Would he relish the attention paid to his life and death? Would he be mortified to learn that today the mysteries surrounding him, his death, and his graves are still debated? *Jesuit Relations 59* tells us of Marquette's final words and actions on earth:

"Then, feeling that he had but a short time to live, he made a last effort, clasped his hands, and, with a steady and fond look upon his crucifix, he uttered aloud his profession of faith, and gave thanks to the divine majesty for the great favor which he had accorded him of dying in the Society, of dying in it as a missionary of Jesus Christ, — and, above all, of dying in it, as he had always prayed, in a wretched cabin in the midst of the forests and bereft of all human succor."[164]

THE END

In the spring of 2022, it was announced that the nineteen purported bone fragments of Father Marquette, once sent to Marquette University, were destined to be again buried in Saint Ignace. A committee consisting of tribal elders, historians, and religious leaders had arranged to retrieve the bone fragments stored for over a hundred years at Marquette University and bury those bones again at the Marquette Mission site. Funds were collected and a documentary was planned. The group called the project *The Return*.

On March 30th, 2022, a group of Native American spiritual leaders and clergy traveled to Marquette University in Milwaukee, Wisconsin. They exchanged gifts, as Marquette once did with the Sioux, in a ceremony with a heavy focus on spiritual and religious tradition. They solemnly transferred the bone fragments from the wrappings which had been their home for nearly 150 years to a birch-bark container.

On June 18th, 2022, the bone fragments were transferred back to the sand from which they came in a festive community celebration. In attendance were townspeople, historians, Jesuits, and representatives of the various tribes Marquette ministered to during his lifetime. Included were members of the Odawa tribe, the tribe responsible for bringing his bones from Ludington to Saint Ignace in 1677. The nineteen bone fragments were placed in a specially constructed birch bark container and interred under a

The Unsolved Mysteries of Father Marquette's Many Graves

limestone slab at the Museum of Ojibwa Culture and Father Marquette Mission Park.

In several media sources, the committee members acknowledge there are lingering questions, but they made no excuses nor attempt to address the doubts. They made no promises of further testing or investigation.

The bones, whether the bones of faithful Marquette, or simply symbols representing his dedication to the Native American people, are a reminder of his kind acts. They symbolize his contributions to the exploration of North America. The bones invoke remembrance of the gentle, understanding passion he possessed.

Is the currently identified Marquette Mission site actually Marquette's burial site? The truth is no one knows if it is or if it isn't. The location of Marquette's Saint Ignace grave is still a matter of debate and investigation should continue. There are several reasons why.

First, a human skeleton weighs 15 to 20 pounds live weight. Marquette's skeleton once contained a dozen bones between 10 to 20 inches long and around 194 other bones. The bone fragments once stored at Marquette University weigh less than one ounce. Even if the nineteen bone fragments are Marquette, there are more bones or clues to find. Remember, the search in 1877 was haphazard. Digging was not orderly.

Why is it important to continue to look? This phrase - archaeological site attrition - succinctly summarizes the fear we should all have. Each year with each rain storm or construction project, minor or hugely important archaeological information erodes or is chiseled away. This is a nonrenewable resource.

Several such events of destruction have already been recorded in this book. In Chapter 18, for example, Jacker

The End

discussed the Murrays revealing they found human remains buried with silk and gold in front of the identified chapel site. Unfortunately, except for one paragraph, the clues regarding this burial are now gone. And the eroding away of important clues continues.

Right after the monument was erected, a combined opera house and general store was put up on part of the lot. An outhouse identified as being part of the opera house complex was constructed on the exact edge of the presumed gravesite. Later, a gas station was built across Marquette Street with underground fuel tanks. Recently, a large hole was dug for a waterline repair on nearby private property. We know the site has been disturbed by farming, looting at the time of Jacker's study, electric, water and sewer lines, the building of the monument, and the moving of the museum building. Each year that goes by inadvertent destruction happens. Ignorance and time will destroy what remains.

Further research shouldn't be feared. With modern technology, it can be completed avoiding invasive techniques. It can either prove or disprove the currently identified site. Either way, we learn more. We interest more people. They learn more. Most importantly, the archaeological remains of this remarkable time period, and perhaps, the rest of the remains of the great priest himself will be safe.

Meanwhile, *The Return* has again evoked excitement in the story of Father Marquette, the history of Saint Ignace, and particularly the unique seventeenth century history of the region. Television and newspaper stories educating the public as to the significance of the Jesuits, the man, and the mysteries of his graves have expanded knowledge. While many of the mysteries of Marquette's graves remain unsolved, one thing that is certain is that the nineteen bone fragments from Marquette University belong in Saint Ignace. If the bone fragments are never proven to be Marquette, the

The Unsolved Mysteries of Father Marquette's Many Graves

retrieval of the bones was still honorable, just, and commendable. After all, the fragments could very well be the bones of Marquette. And if they are the saintly Marquette, it is the only appropriate ending, as it was his dying wish to return to his beloved Mission of Saint Ignace at Michilimackinac.

But is it the end? We will have to see.

FOOTNOTES

[1] There were a couple of unsuccessful attempts to found Jesuit missions in North America prior to 1611. A short lived mission called The Ajacan Mission was built in Virginia in 1570. In 1609, a mission was constructed on Penobscot Bay in Maine. *Jesuit Relations* 71, p. 137, states the Jesuit missionaries established a permanent presence in North America in 1611.

[2] Thwaites, Reuben Gold, ed. *Jesuit Relations and Allied Documents, Travels and Explorations of the Jesuit Missionaries in New France, 1610-1791; The Original French, Latin, and Italian Texts, with English Translations and Notes.* Vol. 34, Burrows Bros., 1896-1901, p. 12. From this point on referenced only as *Jesuit Relations* and the book number.

[3] The Huron are known in Canada as Wendat. In the United States, they were later called the Wyandotte.

[4] *Jesuit Relations 34*, p. 12.

[5] *Jesuit Relations 34*, p. 121.

[6] *Jesuit Relations 34*, pp. 14 and 15.

[7] *Jesuit Relations 42*, pp. 225-245.

[8] Kellogg, Louise Phelps. *The French Regime In Wisconsin And the Northwest.* State Historical Society of Wisconsin, 1925, pp. 147-157.

[9] *Jesuit Relations 1*, p. 32.

[10] Thwaites, Reuben Gold. *Father Marquette.* D. Appleton and Company, 1902, p. 19.

[11] *Jesuit Relations 54*, p. 11.

[12] *Jesuit Relations 55*, p. 131.

[13] *Documents Relative to the Colonial History of the State of New-York: Procured In Holland.* Volume IX, page 304, says 17 tribes joined St. Lusson. On page 383, it says 14 tribes.

[14] The tribes the Jesuits referred to as Algonquin are almost certainly those who call themselves Anishinaabe.

[15] *Proceedings of the Royal Society of Canada: Deliberations et Memoires de la Societe Royale Du Canada.* Royal Society of Canada, 1883, p. 29.

[16] Verwyst, Chrysostom. *Missionary Labors of Fathers Marquette, Menard and Allouez, in the Lake Superior Region.* Hoffman Brothers, 1886, p. 96. Excerpt from a letter written by Edward Jacker to Verwyst.

[17] An account of the deadly skirmish at the mission in Sault Sainte Marie and the burning of the mission house can be found in *Jesuit Relations 58*, pp. 257-261.

[18] *Jesuit Relations 59*, p. 16.

[19] Lahontan, Louis Armand de Lom d'Arce, Baron de. *New Voyages to North-America.* Vol. 1, A.C. McClurg and Co., 1905, p. 149.

[20] O'Callaghan, E. B. (Edmund Bailey), Berthold Fernow, John Romeyn Brodhead, and New York (State) Legislature. *Documents Relative to the*

The Unsolved Mysteries of Father Marquette's Many Graves

Colonial History of the State of New-York: Procured In Holland, England, And France. Weed, Parsons, 1853-1887, Volume IV, pp. 736 and 737.

[21] Rezek, Antoine Ivan. *History of the Diocese of Sault Ste. Marie and Marquette: Containing a Full and Accurate Account of the Development of the Catholic Church in Upper Michigan, with Portraits of Bishops, Priests and Illustrations of Churches Old and New.* Vol. I, Roman Catholic Diocese of Marquette, 1906, p. 342.

[22] Wood, Edwin Orin. *Historic Mackinac: the Historical, Picturesque And Legendary Features of Mackinac Country; Illustrated From Sketches, Drawings, Maps And Photographs, With an Original Map of Mackinac Island, Made Especially for This Work.* The Macmillan Company, 1918, pp. 379 and 549.

[23] *Jesuit Relations 50*, p. 321.

[24] Margry, Pierre. *Decouvertes et Etablissements des Francais Dans L'ouest et Dans le Dud de L'Amerique Septentrionale: Memoires et Documents Inedits.* Maisonneuve, 1879, p. 46.

[25] From the Journal of Dollier and Galinee found in Kellogg, Louise Phelps. *Early Narratives of the Northwest. 1634-1699: With a Facsimile and Two Maps.* Charles Scribner's Sons, 1917, pp. 205 and 206.

[26] Newton, Stanley. *The Story of Sault Ste. Marie and Chippewa County.* Sault News Printing, 1923, pp. 58-70.

[27] Sources are confusing when discussing various people from the seventeenth century and the titles donné or Jesuit Brother. For instance, Louis Le Boesme, one of the men who likely should be credited with building the fort at Sault Saint Marie, was called a Jesuit Brother in some writings and a donné in others.

[28] *Jesuit Relations 59*, p. 243.

[29] From the Journal of Dollier and Galinee found in Kellogg, Louise Phelps. *Early Narratives of the Northwest. 1634-1699: With a Facsimile and Two Maps.* Charles Scribner's Sons, 1917, pp. 205-206.

[30] *Jesuit Relations 54*, p. 127.

[31] *Jesuit Relations 54*, p. 127-129.

[32] *Jesuit Relations 54*, p. 131.

[33] Four English (U. S.) bushels or twelve French bushels of moose guts.

[34] From the Journal of Dollier and Galinee found in Kellogg, Louise Phelps. *Early Narratives of the Northwest. 1634-1699: With a Facsimile and Two Maps.* Charles Scribner's Sons, 1917, p. 207.

[35] *Jesuit Relations 54*, p. 11.

[36] *Jesuit Relations 54*, p. 11.

[37] *Jesuit Relations 54*, p. 131.

[38] *Jesuit Relations 44*, p. 99.

[39] *Jesuit Relations 50*, p. 299.

FOOTNOTES

[40] *Jesuit Relations 54*, p. 165.
[41] *Jesuit Relations 54*, p. 11.
[42] *Jesuit Relations 54*, p. 165.
[43] *Jesuit Relations 54*, p. 165.
[44] *Jesuit Relations 1*, p. 32.
[45] Thwaites, Reuben Gold. "The Story of Chequamegon Bay." *Collections of the State Historical Society of Wisconsin*, Vol. 8, State Historical Society of Wisconsin, 1895, pp. 405-406.
[46] *Jesuit Relations 50*, p. 295 and 297.
[47] *Jesuit Relations 54*, p. 173 and 175.
[48] Verwyst, Chrysostom. *Missionary Labors of Fathers Marquette, Menard and Allouez, in the Lake Superior Region.* Hoffman Brothers, 1886, p. 96.
[49] *Jesuit Relations 54*, p. 169.
[50] *Jesuit Relations 54*, p. 189.
[51] *Jesuit Relations 55*, p. 169.
[52] *Jesuit Relations 55*, p. 95.
[53] *Jesuit Relations 54*, p. 13.
[54] *Jesuit Relations 56*, p. 113. And also Blair, Emma Helen, et al. *The Indian Tribes of the Upper Mississippi Valley and Region of the Great Lakes, as described by Nicolas Perrot..., French Commandant in the Northwest; Bacqueville de la Potherie, French royal commissioner to Canada; Morrell Marston, American army officer; and Thomas Forsyth, United States agent at Fort Armstrong.* The Arthur H. Clark Company, 1911, pp. 187-189.
[55] *Jesuit Relations 56*, p. 113-115.
[56] Hamilton, Raphael N. *Father Marquette.* William B. Eerdman's Publishing Company, 1970, pp. 38-39.
[57] Thwaites, Reuben Gold. "The Story of Chequamegon Bay." *Collections of the State Historical Society of Wisconsin*, Vol. 8, State Historical Society of Wisconsin, 1895, p. 406.
[58] Thwaites, Reuben Gold. "The Story of Chequamegon Bay." *Collections of the State Historical Society of Wisconsin*, Vol. 8, State Historical Society of Wisconsin, 1895, p. 406.
[59] *Jesuit Relations 55*, p. 143.
[60] *Jesuit Relations 57*, p. 241.
[61] *Jesuit Relations 55*, pp. 137 and 139.
[62] Mackinac or Mackinaw, the shortened version of Michilimackinac, wasn't used until much later.
[63] *Jesuit Relations 57*, pp. 219-221.

The Unsolved Mysteries of Father Marquette's Many Graves

[64] Thwaites, Reuben Gold. *Father Marquette*. D. Appleton and Company, 1902, p. 102.
[65] *Jesuit Relations 57*, pp. 205-207.
[66] *Jesuit Relations 55*, p. 107.
[67] *Jesuit Relations 55*, pp. 111-113.
[68] *Jesuit Relations 56*, p. 115.
[69] Blair, Emma Helen, et al. *The Indian Tribes of the Upper Mississippi Valley and Region of the Great Lakes, as described by Nicolas Perrot…, French Commandant in the Northwest; Bacqueville de la Potherie, French royal commissioner to Canada; Morrell Marston, American army officer; and Thomas Forsyth, United States agent at Fort Armstrong.* The Arthur H. Clark Company, 1911, pp. 187-189.
[70] *Jesuit Relations 57*, p. 271.
[71] *Jesuit Relations 59*, p. 227.
[72] *Jesuit Relations 57*, p. 167.
[73] *Jesuit Relations 57*, p. 169.
[74] Lahontan, Louis Armand de Lom d'Arce, Baron de. *Travels in Canada*. Longman, Hurst, Rees, and Orme, 1808, p. 284.
[75] Thwaites, Reuben Gold. "The Story of Chequamegon Bay." *Collections of the State Historical Society of Wisconsin*, Vol. 8, State Historical Society of Wisconsin, 1895, p. 438. Statements by Father Allouez.
[76] *Jesuit Relations 57*, pp. 261 and 263.
[77] *Jesuit Relations 59*, p. 89.
[78] Hedges, Samuel. *Father Marquette: Jesuit Missionary and Explorer, the Discoverer of the Mississippi. His Place of Burial at St. Ignace, Michigan.* Christian Press Association, 1903, p. 9.
[79] *Jesuit Relations 59*, pp. 89 and 91.
[80] *Jesuit Relations 59*, pp. 93 and 95.
[81] *Jesuit Relations 59*, p. 95.
[82] *Jesuit Relations 59*, p. 97.
[83] *Jesuit Relations 59*, p. 111.
[84] *Jesuit Relations 59*, p. 121.
[85] Blair, Emma Helen, et al. *The Indian Tribes of the Upper Mississippi Valley and Region of the Great Lakes, as described by Nicolas Perrot…, French Commandant in the Northwest; Bacqueville de la Potherie, French royal commissioner to Canada; Morrell Marston, American army officer; and Thomas Forsyth, United States agent at Fort Armstrong.* The Arthur H. Clark Company, 1911, pp. 186-189.
[86] Ibid.
[87] *Jesuit Relations 59*, p. 131.
[88] *Jesuit Relations 54*, p. 191.

FOOTNOTES

[89] *Jesuit Relations 58*, p. 99.

[90] *Jesuit Relations 58*, p. 91.

[91] O'Callaghan, E. B. (Edmund Bailey), Berthold Fernow, John Romeyn Brodhead, and New York (State) Legislature. *Documents Relative to the Colonial History of the State of New-York: Procured In Holland, England, And France*. Vol. IX, Weed, Parsons, 1853-1887, p. 121.

[92] The account of the deadly skirmish at the mission in Sault Sainte Marie and the burning of the mission house is from *Jesuit Relations 58*, pp. 257-261.

[93] *Jesuit Relations 58*, pp. 259-261.

[94] Margry, Pierre. *Decouvertes et Etablissements des Francais Dans L'ouest et Dans le Sud de L'Amerique Septentrionale (1614-1754): Memoires et Documents Inedits*. Vol. 1, Imprimerie D. Jouaust, 1776, pp. 322 and 367.

[95] *Jesuit Relations 42*, p. 263.

[96] Winsor, Justin. *Narrative and Critical History of America, French Explorations and Settlements in North America and Those of the Portuguese, Dutch, and Swedes 1500-1700*. Vol. 4, The Riverside Press, 1884, p. 176. And also, Warren, William Whipple. *History of the Ojibways: Based Upon Traditions and Oral Statements*. Vol. 5, Minnesota Historical Society, 1885, pp. 408-409.

[97] Minnesota Historical Society. *The Aborigines of Minnesota: A Report Based on the Collections of Jacob V. Brower, and on the Field Surveys and Notes of Alfred J. Hill and Theodore H. Lewis*. The Pioneer Co., 1911, p. 524.

[98] *Jesuit Relations 59*, p. 71.

[99] Warren, William Whipple. *History of the Ojibways: Based Upon Traditions and Oral Statements*. Vol. 5, Minnesota Historical Society, 1885, pp. 408-409.

[100] *Jesuit Relations 58*, p. 107.

[101] Gagnon, Ernest. *Louis Jolliet, Decouvreur du Mississippi et du Pays des Illinois, Premier Seigneur de l'île D'Anticosti*. No Publisher, 1902, p. 89. Quote from handwritten letter by Joliet dated 10 October 1674.

[102] *Jesuit Relations 59*, p. 185.

[103] *Jesuit Relations 59*, pp. 187-189.

[104] *Jesuit Relations 59*, p. 191.

[105] Rochemonteix, Camille. *Les Jesuites Et La Nouvelle-France Au XVIIe Siecle D'apres Beaucoup De Documents Inedits Par Le P. Camille De Rochemonteix*. Vol. 3, Letouzey et Ane, 1896, pp. 606-612. Letter from Jesuit Pierre Cholenec to R. P. Fontenay which was dated October 10, 1675. It specifically says that Marquette was summoned to Michilimackinac to attend a gathering of the Jesuits.

[106] *Jesuit Relations 59*, pp. 191-193.

[107] *Jesuit Relations 59*, p. 205.

The Unsolved Mysteries of Father Marquette's Many Graves

[108] Thwaites, Reuben Gold. "The Story of Chequamegon Bay." *Collections of the State Historical Society of Wisconsin*, Vol. 8, State Historical Society of Wisconsin, 1895, pp. 437-438. Allouez talking about his hardships in "The Story of Chequamegon Bay" by Thwaites.

[109] *Jesuit Relations 59*, p. 201.

[110] Charlevoix, Pierre Francois Xavier. *Journal of A Voyage to North America, I and II*. Vol. 2, R. and J. Dodsley, 1761, pp. 72-73.

[111] Hubbard, Gurdon S. *Pioneer Collections: Report of the Pioneer Society of the State of Michigan*. Vol. 3, Pioneer Society of State of Michigan, 1903, p. 126. Statements by Gurdon S. Hubbard, Clerk for the American Fur Trading Company.

[112] Defining L'Arbre Croche as used in historic texts is problematic as the name was used to describe an area along Lake Michigan stretching between what is now known as Cross Village, Michigan and Harbor Springs, Michigan.

[113] *History of Mason County, Michigan: With Illustrations and Biographical Sketches of Some of Its Prominent Men and Pioneers*. H. R. Page & Co., 1882, p. 8. This quote likely dates from the mid- 1840s.

[114] "Father Marquette's Bones: Believed to Have Been Found Near Frankfort, Michigan." *Indianapolis News*, 25 Dec. 1900, Evening Edition, Volume 32, Number 16, John H. Holliday, p. 1.

[115] Duffield, George. *Pioneer Collections: Report of the Pioneer Society of the State of Michigan*. Vol. 2, Pioneer Society of State of Michigan, 1880, p. 140.

[116] Wright, John C. *The Crooked Tree, Indian Legends of Northern Michigan*. Thunder Bay Press, 1917, p. 165.

[117] Dionne, Narcisse-Eutrope. *Gabriel Richard: Sulpicien, Cure Et Second Fondateur De La Ville De Detroit; La Memoire Du P. Rasle Vengee*. Typ. Laflamme & Proulx, 1911, p. 45. Says Marquette was the founder of Michilimackinac and L'Arbre Croche.

[118] *Concerning the Death and Burial of Father Jacques Marquette, S. J. and of the Rediscovery of His Grave*. Marquette Mission Park and Museum of Ojibwa Culture, 1990, p. 6.

[119] Various sources report different sizes, but all reported sizes vary by less than 6 feet in either direction.

[120] Rezek, Antoine Ivan. *History of the Diocese of Sault Ste. Marie and Marquette: Containing a Full and Accurate Account of the Development of the Catholic Church in Upper Michigan, with Portraits of Bishops, Priests and Illustrations of Churches Old and New*. Vol. II, Roman Catholic Diocese of Marquette, 1907, pp. 127 and 128.

[121] Rezek, Antoine Ivan. *History of the Diocese of Sault Ste. Marie and Marquette: Containing a Full and Accurate Account of the Development of the Catholic Church in Upper Michigan, with Portraits of Bishops,*

Footnotes

Priests and Illustrations of Churches Old and New. Vol. II, Roman Catholic Diocese of Marquette, 1907, p. 128.

[122] "The Recent Discoveries at St. Ignace: Shall We or Shall We Not Recover the Bones of Marquette." *Pioneer Collections: Report of the Pioneer Society of the State of Michigan*, Vol. 2, Pioneer Society of State of Michigan, 1880, p. 142. Credited within the text to the Sault Evening News in 1877.

[123] Holzknecht, J. "The Relics of Pere Marquette." *The American Catholic Historical Researches*, Volume 12, No. 1, American Catholic Historical Society, 1895, p. 30.

[124] *History of the Upper Peninsula of Michigan: Containing a Full Account of Its Early Settlement, Its Growth, Development, and Resources, an Extended Description of Its Iron and Copper Mines: Also, Accurate Sketches of Its Counties, Cities, Towns, and Villages, Their Improvements, Industries, Manufactories, Biographical Sketches, Portraits of Prominent Men and Early Settlers, Views of County Seats, Etc.* The Western Historical Company, 1883, pp. 367-368.

[125] Shea, John Gilmary. "The Romance and Reality of the Death of Father James Marquette, and the Recent Discovery of His Remains." *Catholic World*, Vol. 26, The Catholic Publication Society, 1877/1878, p. 276.

[126] Various sources report between 35 and 39 pieces were found in total. Jacker stated thirty-five, thirty-six, thirty-seven, and thirty-nine in different texts.

[127] Hedges, Samuel. *Father Marquette: Jesuit Missionary and Explorer, the Discoverer of the Mississippi. His Place of Burial at St. Ignace, Michigan.* Christian Press Association, 1903, pp. 133-134.

[128] Verwyst, Chrysostom. *Missionary Labors of Fathers Marquette, Menard and Allouez, in the Lake Superior Region.* Hoffman Brothers, 1886, p. 141. Excerpt from a letter written by Edward Jacker to Verwyst.

[129] *Concerning the Death and Burial of Father Jacques Marquette, S. J. and of the Rediscovery of His Grave.* Marquette Mission Park and Museum of Ojibwa Culture, 1990, p. 7.

[130] Hedges, Samuel. *Father Marquette: Jesuit Missionary and Explorer, the Discoverer of the Mississippi. His Place of Burial at St. Ignace, Michigan.* Christian Press Association, 1903, p. 121.

[131] Lahontan, Louis Armand de Lom d'Arce, Baron de. *New Voyages to North-America.* Vol. 1, A.C. McClurg and Co., 1905, p. 146. From a letter dated 5/26/1688 from Michilimackinac.

[132] *Concerning the Death and Burial of Father Jacques Marquette, S. J. and of the Rediscovery of His Grave.* Marquette Mission Park and Museum of Ojibwa Culture, 1990, p. 16.

[133] Hedges, Samuel. *Father Marquette: Jesuit Missionary and Explorer, the Discoverer of the Mississippi. His Place of Burial at St. Ignace, Michigan.* Christian Press Association, 1903, pp. 149-150.

The Unsolved Mysteries of Father Marquette's Many Graves

[134] Hedges, Samuel. *Father Marquette: Jesuit Missionary and Explorer, the Discoverer of the Mississippi. His Place of Burial at St. Ignace, Michigan.* Christian Press Association, 1903, pp. 147-149.

[135] Charlevoix, Pierre Francois Xavier. *Journal of A Voyage to North America, I and II.* Vol. 2, R. and J. Dodsley, 1761, p. 31.

[136] Jacker, Edward. *Father Edward Jacker's Account of the Discovery of the Grave of Father Marquette.* Michilimackinac Historical Society, 1977, p. 6.

[137] *Jesuit Relations 56*, p. 11.

[138] Hedges, Samuel. *Father Marquette: Jesuit Missionary and Explorer, the Discoverer of the Mississippi. His Place of Burial at St. Ignace, Michigan.* Christian Press Association, 1903, pp. 155-156.

[139] *Jesuit Relations 59*, p. 205.

[140] Verwyst, Chrysostom. *Missionary Labors of Fathers Marquette, Menard and Allouez, in the Lake Superior Region.* Hoffman Brothers, 1886, p. 136. Excerpt from a letter written by Edward Jacker to Verwyst.

[141] Verwyst, Chrysostom. *Missionary Labors of Fathers Marquette, Menard and Allouez, in the Lake Superior Region.* Hoffman Brothers, 1886, p. 137. Excerpt from a letter written by Edward Jacker to Verwyst.

[142] It's not clear if the burial found by Murray with silk and gold trimmed clothing was on the lakeside of the purported Marquette grave site or on the Marquette Street side (south).

[143] There was a Catholic Church and cemetery at the corner of McCann and South State Street. The Catholic church was built in 1837. It replaced a log church that was located behind it. The 1837 church was later moved to the Marquette Mission site; however, it is not the original mission church from the 1600s. There was a cemetery on McCann Street that could have slightly predated the 1830s; however, statements have been found supporting the fact that this was the only recorded post-contact cemetery downtown. When the 1837 mission church was moved and converted to a museum, some of the artifacts intended for the museum's use were those found during the Jacker exploration.

[144] Seeman, Eric R. *Death in the New World: Cross-Cultural Encounters.* University of Pennsylvania Press, 2011, p. 136.

[145] Shea, John Gilmary. "The Romance and Reality of the Death of Father James Marquette, and the Recent Discovery of His Remains." *Catholic World*, The Catholic Publication Society, Vol. 26, 1877/1878, pp. 278-279.

[146] Brown, Edward Osgood. "Marquette at Michillimackinac." *Chicago Historical Society: Report of Special Meeting, April 3, 1900*, Chicago Historical Society, 1900, p. 268. Excerpt from a letter written by Jacker to Shea.

FOOTNOTES

[147] Verwyst, Chrysostom. *Missionary Labors of Fathers Marquette, Menard and Allouez, in the Lake Superior Region.* Hoffman Brothers, 1886, p. 143. Excerpt from a letter written by Edward Jacker to Verwyst.

[148] Hurlbut, Henry Higgins. *Father Marquette at Mackinaw and Chicago: A Paper, Read Before the Chicago Historical Society.* Jansen, McClurg, & Co., 1878, p. 8.

[149] Holzknecht, J. "The Relics of Pere Marquette." *The American Catholic Historical Researches*, Volume 12, No. 1, American Catholic Historical Society, 1895, pp. 30-31.

[150] Spalding, H. S. "The Grave and Relics of Father Marquette." *The Messenger of the Sacred Heart of Jesus*, Vol. 36, The Apostleship of Prayer, 1901, p. 168.

[151] Ibid.

[152] Weadock, Thomas. "Pere Marquette, The Missionary Explorer." *Pioneer Collections: Report of the Pioneer Society of the State of Michigan*, Vol. 21, Pioneer Society of State of Michigan, 1894, p. 464.

[153] Verwyst, Chrysostom. *Missionary Labors of Fathers Marquette, Menard and Allouez, in the Lake Superior Region.* Hoffman Brothers, 1886, p. 143. Excerpt from a letter written by Edward Jacker to Verwyst.

[154] Cardinal, Jane. "Father Marquette's Remains: Another Record of the Discovery." *Mackinac Journal*, May 2017, Gatehouse Media, 2017, p. 46.

[155] Holzknecht, J. "The Relics of Pere Marquette." *The American Catholic Historical Researches*, Volume 12, No. 1, American Catholic Historical Society, 1895, p. 30.

[156] *Concerning the Death and Burial of Father Jacques Marquette, S. J. and of the Rediscovery of His Grave.* Marquette Mission Park and Museum of Ojibwa Culture, 1990, p. 17.

[157] "Historical Interest in Murray Obituary: Father Marquette's Grave Found on her Property." *Green Bay Press Gazette.* 14 June 1935, p. 10. Expanded version of an obituary published in *The Republican News and St. Ignace Enterprise* on June 13, 1935.

[158] Sweeney, Ann. "OK, Who Stole Marquette's Bones?" *The Detroit News*, Volume 326, 14 July 1985, pp. 1G and 6G.

[159] Schacher, Dr. Susan. Letter to Dr. Doug Sadler. 23 November 1989. Michigan Vertical File (Third Floor), Special Collections. Kenneth J. Shouldice Library, Lake Superior State University, Sault Sainte Marie, Michigan.

[160] Cleland, Dr. Charles. "Testimony of Dr. Charles Cleland on Behalf of the Bay Mills Indian Community In the Matter the Application of Enbridge... for Authority to Replace and Relocated the Segment of Line 5 Crossing the Straits of Mackinac into a Tunnel, etc." Case No. U-20763, Michigan Public Service Commission, 14 September 2021. Direct Testimony.

The Unsolved Mysteries of Father Marquette's Many Graves

[161] Maidenberg, Michael. "State Archaeologists Try to Rescue Historical Sites." *Detroit Free Press,* Sunday Edition, Volume 142 - No. 49, 25 June 1972, p. 39.

[162] Fitting, James E. "St. Ignace in the 19th Century: Information from Archaeological Remains." *Toledo Area Aboriginal Research Bulletin,* Vol. 4, No. 2, 1975, p. 2. Held at the University of Wisconsin - Madison Libraries. Used with permission of the Toledo Area Aboriginal Research Society.

[163] Steck, Francis Borgia. *Marquette Legends.* Pageant Press, 1960, p. xv.

[164] *Jesuit Relations 59,* p. 197.

REFERENCES AND WORKS CITED

Arbic, Bernie. *City of the Rapids*. The Priscilla Press, 2003.

Baraga, Frederic. *A Dictionary of the Otchipwe Language, Explained in English*. Beauchemin & Valois, 1878, p. 238.

Blair, Emma Helen, et al. *The Indian Tribes of the Upper Mississippi Valley and Region of the Great Lakes, as described by Nicolas Perrot..., French Commandant in the Northwest; Bacqueville de la Potherie, French royal commissioner to Canada; Morrell Marston, American army officer; and Thomas Forsyth*, United States agent at Fort Armstrong. The Arthur H. Clark Company, 1911, pp. 186-189.

Blanchard, Rufus. *Discovery and Conquests of the North-west: with the History of Chicago*. Part 6, Cushing, Thomas, and Company, 1880, p. 11.

Branstner, Susan. *Calumet & Fleur-de-lys: Archaeology of Indian and French Contact in the Midcontinent*. Smithsonian, 1992. (Susan Branstner is aka Dr. Susan Schacher)

Branstner, Susan. [Private correspondence]. St. Ignace (Mich.) Folder - Archaeology - Marquette Mission, File 1-7. Special Collections, Kenneth J. Shouldice Library, Lake Superior State University, Sault Sainte Marie, Michigan. (Susan Branstner is aka Dr. Susan Schacher)

Brown, Edward Osgood. "Marquette at Michillimackinac." *Chicago Historical Society: Report of Special Meeting, April 3, 1900*, Chicago Historical Society, 1900, pp. 264-272.

Brown, Edward Osgood. *Two Missionary Priests at Mackinac*. Barnard & Gunthorp, 1889.

Cardinal, Jane. "Father Marquette's Remains: Another Record of the Discovery." *Mackinac Journal*, May 2017, Gatehouse Media, 2017, p. 46.

Charlevoix, Pierre Francois Xavier. *Journal of A Voyage to North America, I and II*. Vol. 2, R. and J. Dodsley, 1761, pp. 31, 72-73.

Concerning the Death and Burial of Father Jacques Marquette, S. J. and of the Rediscovery of His Grave. Marquette Mission Park and Museum of Ojibwa Culture, 1990, pp. 6-17.

Costain, Thomas B. *The White and the Gold: The French Regime in Canada*. Doubleday, 1954, p. 358.

Davidson, J. N. *Missions on Chequamegon Bay*. Democrat Printing Company, 1892, p. 436.

Deangelis, Jean. *Life and Voyages of Louis Joliet*. Institute of Jesuit History, 1948, entire.

Deangelis, Jean. "Louis Joliet: the Early Years." *Mid America: An Historical Quarterly*, Vol. XXVII, Institute of Jesuit History, 1945, pp. 3-29.

The Unsolved Mysteries of Father Marquette's Many Graves

Dionne, Narcisse-Eutrope. *Gabriel Richard: Sulpicien, Curé Et Second Fondateur De La Ville De Détroit; La Mémoire Du P. Rasle Vengée.* Typ. Laflamme & Proulx, 1911, p. 45.

Duffield, George. *Pioneer Collections: Report of the Pioneer Society of the State of Michigan.* Vol. 2, Pioneer Society of State of Michigan, 1880, p. 140.

"Father Marquette, S. J.: The Discovery of His Remains." *Woodstock Letters: A Record of Current Events and Historical Notes Connected with the Colleges and Missions of the Society of Jesus in North and South America*, Vol. 6, Number 3, Woodstock College, 1877, pp. 159-172. Containing personal correspondence written by Jacker dated 6/13/1877.

"Father Marquette's Bones: Believed to Have Been Found Near Frankfort, Michigan." *Indianapolis News*, 25 Dec. 1900, Evening Edition, Volume 32, Number 16, John H. Holliday, p. 1.

Fitting, James E. "St. Ignace in the 19th Century: Information from Archaeological Remains." *Toledo Area Aboriginal Research Bulletin*, Vol. 4, No. 2, 1975, p. 2. Held at the University of Wisconsin - Madison Libraries. Used with permission of the Toledo Area Aboriginal Research Society.

From The Story of Finding His Grave, as Related by My Mother Mrs. Jane Murray and Widow of Patrick Murray. [Archival material]. St. Ignace (Mich.) Folder - Archaeology-Marquette Mission, File 4. Special Collections, Kenneth J. Shouldice Library, Lake Superior State University, Sault Sainte Marie, Michigan.

Gagnon, Ernest. *Louis Jolliet, Decouvreur du Mississippi et du pays des Illinois, Premier Seigneur de l'île d'Anticosti.* No Publisher, 1902, p. 89. Quote from handwritten letter by Joliet dated October 10, 1674.

Hamilton, Raphael N. *Father Marquette.* William B. Eerdman's Publishing Company, 1970, entire.

Hedges, Samuel. *Father Marquette: Jesuit Missionary and Explorer, the Discoverer of the Mississippi, His Place of Burial at St. Ignace, Michigan.* Christian Press Association, 1903, pp. 9, 86, 99-101, 121, 133, 134, 135, 147-150, 155-156.

Heldman, Donald P. "Euro-American Archaeology in Michigan: The French Period." *Retrieving Michigan's Buried Past: The Archaeology of the Great Lakes State*, Cranbrook Institute, 1999, p. 295.

"Historical Interest In Murray Obituary: Father Marquette's Grave Found On Her Property." *Green Bay Press Gazette*, 14 June 1935, p. 10. Expanded version of an obituary published in *The Enterprise* on June 13, 1935.

History of Mason County, Michigan: With Illustrations and Biographical Sketches of Some of Its Prominent Men and Pioneers. H. R. Page & Co., 1882, p. 8. This quote likely dates from the mid-1840s.

REFERENCES AND WORKS CITED

History of the Upper Peninsula of Michigan: Containing a Full Account of Its Early Settlement, Its Growth, Development, and Resources, an Extended Description of Its Iron and Copper Mines: Also, Accurate Sketches of Its Counties, Cities, Towns, and Villages, Their Improvements, Industries, Manufactories, Biographical Sketches, Portraits of Prominent Men and Early Settlers, Views of County Seats, Etc. The Western Historical Company, 1883, pp. 367-368.

Holzknecht, J. "The Relics of Pere Marquette." *The American Catholic Historical Researches*, Volume 12, No. 1, American Catholic Historical Society, 1895, p. 30-31.

Hubbard, Gurdon S. *Pioneer Collections: Report of the Pioneer Society of the State of Michigan.* Vol. 3, Pioneer Society of State of Michigan, 1903, p. 126. Statements by Gurdon S. Hubbard, Clerk for the American Fur Trading Company.

Hubbard, Gurdon Saltonstall and Caroline Margaret McIlvaine. *The Autobiography of Gurdon Saltonstall Hubbard: Pa-pa-ma-ta-be, "The Swift Walker".* R.R. Donnelley, 1911, pp. 31 and 32.

Hurlbut, Henry Higgins. *Father Marquette at Mackinaw and Chicago: A Paper, Read Before the Chicago Historical Society.* Jansen, McClurg, & Co., 1878, p. 8.

Jacker, Edward. *Father Edward Jacker's Account of the Discovery of the Grave of Father Marquette.* Michilimackinac Historical Society, 1977, pp. 6-8.

Kellogg, Louise Phelps. *Early Narratives of the Northwest.* C. Scribners's Sons, 1917, pp. 30-32, 205-206. Contained within is the Journal of Dollier and Galinee.

Kellogg, Louise Phelps. *The French Regime In Wisconsin And the Northwest.* State Historical Society of Wisconsin, 1925, pp. 114-117, 147-157.

Kelton, Dwight H. *Annals of Fort Mackinac.* Detroit Free Press, 1886.

Keul, J. A. "Antique Reminiscences of Saint Ignace." *Saint Ignace Enterprise: Woman's Edition*, Saint Ignace Enterprise, 1897, n. p.

Lahontan, Louis Armand de Lom d'Arce, Baron de. *New Voyages to North-America.* Vol. 1, A.C. McClurg and Co., 1905, pp. 146-149.

Lahontan, Louis Armand de Lom d'Arce, Baron de. *Travels in Canada.* Longman, Hurst, Rees, and Orme, 1808, p. 284.

Maidenberg, Michael. "State Archaeologists Try to Rescue Historical Sites." *Detroit Free Press*, Sunday Edition, Vol. 142 - No. 49, 25 June 1972, p. 39.

Margry, Pierre. *Decouvertes et Etablissements des Francais Dans L'ouest et Dans le Sud de L'Amerique Septentrionale.* Imprimerie D. Jouaust, 1776, Vol. 1, pp. 322 and 367.

The Unsolved Mysteries of Father Marquette's Many Graves

Margry, Pierre. *Decouvertes et Etablissements des Francais Dans L'ouest et Dans le Sud de L'Amerique Septentrionale: Memoires et Documents Inedits*. Maisonneuve, 1879, p. 46.

[Marquette Mission Park and Museum of Ojibwa Culture: St. Ignace]. 1982-1991. Michigan Vertical File (Third Floor), Special Collections. Kenneth J. Shouldice Library, Lake Superior State University, Sault Sainte Marie, Michigan.

[Marquette Mission Site Archaeological Digs: Reports and Papers]. 1971-1988. Michigan Vertical File (Third Floor), Special Collections. Kenneth J. Shouldice Library, Lake Superior State University, Sault Sainte Marie, Michigan.

Mast, Dolorita. *Gabriel Richard: Always the Priest: The Life of Gabriel Richard*. Helicon Press, Inc., 1965, p. 184.

McGraw, Jennifer. *Lawless Mackinac*. Pine Stump Publications, 2011.

Minnesota Historical Society. *The Aborigines of Minnesota: A Report Based on the Collections of Jacob V. Brower, and on the Field Surveys and Notes of Alfred J. Hill and Theodore H. Lewis*. The Pioneer Co, 1911, p. 524.

Newton, Stanley. *Mackinac Island and Sault St. Marie*. Soo Evening News, 1923, p. 140.

Newton, Stanley. *The Story of Sault Ste. Marie and Mackinac*. Soo Evening News, 1923, pp. 58 and 70.

Noonan, Herbert C. "250th Anniversary of Marquette's Arrival at Chicago." *Illinois Catholic Historical Review*, Vol. 7, Number 1, Illinois Catholic Historical Society, 1924, pp. 195-226.

O'Callaghan, E. B., Berthold Fernow, John Romeyn Brodhead, and New York State Legislature. *Documents Relative to the Colonial History of the State of New-York: Procured In Holland, England, And France*. Vol. IV, Weed, Parsons, pp. 736 and 737.

O'Callaghan, E. B., Berthold Fernow, John Romeyn Brodhead, and New York State Legislature. *Documents Relative to the Colonial History of the State of New-York: Procured In Holland, England, And France*. Vol. IX, Weed, Parsons, pp. 12, 121, 142, 304, 383, and 793.

Ontario History Scholarly Journal of The Ontario Historical Society Since 1899 Papers and Records. Vol. IV, The Ontario Historical Society, 1903, p. 69.

"Pottowattomy Indians." *Woodstock Letters: A Record of Current Events and Historical Notes Connected with the Colleges and Missions of the Society of Jesus in North and South America*. Vol. 4, Number 1, Woodstock College, 1875, p. 44.

References and Works Cited

Proceedings of the Royal Society of Canada: Deliberations et Memoires de la Societe Royale Du Canada. Royal Society of Canada, 1883, p. 29.

"Recent Discoveries of the Relics of St. Jean de Brebeuf." *Woodstock Letters. A Record of Current Events and Historical Notes Connected with the Colleges and Missions of the Society of Jesus in North and South America*. Vol. 84, Number 1, Woodstock College, 1955, pp. 49-53.

"The Recent Discoveries at St. Ignace: Shall We or Shall We Not Recover the Bones of Marquette." *Pioneer Collections: Report of the Pioneer Society of the State of Michigan*, Vol. 2, Pioneer Society of State of Michigan, 1880, p. 142. Credited within the text to the Sault Evening News in 1877.

Repplier, Agnes. *Pere Marquette: Priest, Pioneer and Adventurer*. Doubleday, Doran, Incorporated, 1929.

Rezek, Antoine Ivan. *History of the Diocese of Sault Ste. Marie and Marquette: Containing a Full and Accurate Account of the Development of the Catholic Church in Upper Michigan, with Portraits of Bishops, Priests and Illustrations of Churches Old and New*. Vol. I, Roman Catholic Diocese of Marquette, 1906, pp. 342, 378, and 379.

Rezek, Antoine Ivan. *History of the Diocese of Sault Ste. Marie and Marquette: Containing a Full and Accurate Account of the Development of the Catholic Church in Upper Michigan, with Portraits of Bishops, Priests and Illustrations of Churches Old and New*. Vol. II, Roman Catholic Diocese of Marquette, 1907, pp. 127 and 128.

Rochemonteix, Camille. *Les Jesuites Et La Nouvelle-France Au XVIIe Siecle D'apres Beaucoup De Documents Inedits Par Le P. Camille De Rochemonteix*. Vol. 3, Letouzey et Ane, 1896, pp. 606-612. Letter from Jesuit Pierre Cholenec to R. P. Fontenay in Nantes which was dated October 10, 1675.

[St. Ignace, Michigan.]. 1971. Michigan Vertical File (Third Floor), Special Collections. Kenneth J. Shouldice Library, Lake Superior State University, Sault Sainte Marie, Michigan.

Schacher, Dr. Susan. Letter to Dr. Doug Sadler. 23 November 1989. Michigan Vertical File (Third Floor), Special Collections. Kenneth J. Shouldice Library, Lake Superior State University, Sault Sainte Marie, Michigan.

Seeman, Eric R. *Death in the New World: Cross-Cultural Encounters*. University of Pennsylvania Press, 2011, pp. 117 and 136.

Shea, John Gilmary. *Discovery of the Exploration of the Mississippi Valley With the Original Narratives of Marquette, Allouez, Membre, Hennepin, and Anastase Douay*. J. S. Redfield, 1853, pp. 57-66.

Shea, John Gilmary. "The Romance and Reality of the Death of Father James Marquette, and the Recent Discovery of His Remains." *Catholic*

The Unsolved Mysteries of Father Marquette's Many Graves

World, The Catholic Publication Society, Vol. 26, 1877/1878, pp. 276-279.

Shurtleff, Mary Belle. *Old Arbre Croche: a Factual And Comprehensive History of Cross Village, Michigan*. 1963, p. 12.

Smith, Emerson. *Before the Bridge*. Kiwanis Club of Saint Ignace, Michigan, 1957.

Spalding, H. S. "The Grave and Relics of Father Marquette." *The Messenger of the Sacred Heart of Jesus*, Vol. 36, The Apostleship of Prayer, 1901, pp. 165-168.

"The Statue of Father Marquette in the National Capital." *Woodstock Letters: A Record of Current Events and Historical Notes Connected with the Colleges and Missions of the Society of Jesus in North and South America*, Vol. 25, Number 1, Woodstock College, 1896, pp. 467-494.

Steck, Francis Borgia. *Marquette Legends*. Pageant Press, 1960, p. xv.

Stone, Lyle M. *Archaeological Investigation of the Marquette Mission Site, St. Ignace, Michigan, 1971: a Preliminary Report*. Mackinac Island State Park Commission, 1972.

Strickland, William Peter. *Old Mackinaw, or, the Fortress of the Lakes and It's Surroundings*. James Challen and Son, 1860, p. 57.

Sweeney, Ann. "OK, Who Stole Marquette's Bones?" *The Detroit News*, Vol. 326, 14 July 1985, pp. 1G and 6G.

Thompson, Joseph J. "History of the Illinois." *Illinois Catholic Historical Review*, Vol. 7, Number 1, Illinois Catholic Historical Society, 1924, p. 249.

Thwaites, Reuben Gold. *Father Marquette*. D. Appleton and Company, 1902, pp. 19 and 102.

Thwaites, Reuben Gold, ed. *Jesuit Relations and Allied Documents, Travels and Explorations of the Jesuit Missionaries in New France, 1610-1791; The Original French, Latin, and Italian Texts, with English Translations and Notes*. 73 Volumes, Burrows Bros., 1896-1901.

Thwaites, Reuben Gold. "The Story of Chequamegon Bay." *Collections of the State Historical Society of Wisconsin*, Vol. 8, State Historical Society of Wisconsin, 1895, pp. 397-440.

Verwyst, Chrysostom. "Life and Labors of Bishop Baraga: A Short Sketch of the Life and Labors of Bishop Baraga - The Great Indian Apostle of the Northwest." *Pioneer Collections: Report of the Pioneer Society of the State of Michigan*, Vol. 26, Pioneer Society of State of Michigan, 1896, p. 539.

Verwyst, Chrysostom. *Missionary Labors of Fathers Marquette, Menard and Allouez, in the Lake Superior Region*. Hoffman Brothers, 1886, pp. 96, 136, 137, 141, and 143.

References and Works Cited

Warren, William Whipple. *History of the Ojibways: Based Upon Traditions and Oral Statements.* Vol. 5, Minnesota Historical Society, 1885, pp. 405-409.

Weadock, Thomas. "Pere Marquette, The Missionary Explorer." *Pioneer Collections: Report of the Pioneer Society of the State of Michigan*, Vol. 21, Pioneer Society of State of Michigan, 1894, pp. 451 and 464.

Winsor, Justin. *Narrative and Critical History of America, French Explorations and Settlements in North America and Those of the Portuguese, Dutch, and Swedes 1500-1700.* Vol. 4, The Riverside Press, 1884, p. 176.

Wood, Edwin Orin. *Historic Mackinac: the Historical, Picturesque And Legendary Features of the Mackinac Country; Illustrated From Sketches, Drawings, Maps And Photographs, With an Original Map of Mackinac Island, Made Especially for This Work.* The Macmillan Company, 1918, pp. 379 and 549.

Wright, John C. *The Crooked Tree, Indian Legends of Northern Michigan.* Thunder Bay Press, 1917, p. 165.

Wright, John C. *The Ottawan: A Short History of the Villages and Resorts Surrounding.* R. Smith and Co., 1895, p. 55.

For additional copies contact:

Pine Stump Publications
W1413 Cheeseman Road
St. Ignace, Michigan 49781